Praise for
FEDERER AND ME

"[Skidelsky] situates the Swiss in historical context, describing him as simultaneously a throwback to traditional tennis and an avatar of modern technology and training. . . . He'll certainly get no argument from the Fed-heads when he observes that the contemporary game of relentless baseline retrieving is boring compared with their man's graceful, instinctive construction of points."

—*The Washington Post*

"The author is at his best when describing Federer's skill and innovation, and fans of the player will likely not dispute the assertions of his grace on court."

—Amanda Mastrull, *Library Journal* (starred review)

"With his careful attention to the evolving talent of Federer and the debates around surface, rackets, strategy matches, and celebrity, Skidelsky scores."

—*Publishers Weekly*

"Skidelsky is excellent at deconstructing the appeal of Federer. . . . This is the kind of book that sports fans will read over the summer, sitting in their gardens or in the stands of the All England Club, with a bowl of strawberries near at hand. It is gentle and wise, discursive but pointed."

—Matthew Syed, *The Times*

"Skidelsky . . . knows that Federer's tennis is more than just Federer's tennis; but for him it is not a metaphor, rather something which has been absorbed into the texture and meaning of his own life."

—Booker Prize–winning author Julian Barnes,
The Guardian

"Thought-provoking, instructive, and highly readable. Positively gripping."

—Simon O'Hagan, *The Independent*

"With clarity he illuminates the champion's striking position as both a preserver and innovator of the sport."

—Laurence Scott, *Financial Times*

"Compelling. Its excellent chapters on the technical changes in the game, the rivalry with Nadal, and the relationship between sport and beauty are well worth the admission money."

—Simon Barnes, *Newsweek*

"Brave . . . engaging . . . ultimately poignant."

—Edmund Gordon, *The Spectator*

FEDERER AND ME

A STORY OF OBSESSION

William Skidelsky

WASHINGTON SQUARE PRESS

— ATRIA —

NEW YORK   LONDON   TORONTO   SYDNEY   NEW DELHI

WASHINGTON SQUARE PRESS

ATRIA

An Imprint of Simon & Schuster, Inc.
1230 Avenue of the Americas
New York, NY 10020

First Washington Square Press/Atria Paperback edition May 2017
First published in Great Britain in 2015 by Yellow Jersey Press

WASHINGTON SQUARE PRESS/ATRIA PAPERBACK and colophon are trademarks of Simon & Schuster, Inc.

For information about special discounts for bulk purchases, please contact Simon & Schuster Special Sales at 1-866-506-1949 or business@simonandschuster.com.

The Simon & Schuster Speakers Bureau can bring authors to your live event. For more information, or to book an event, contact the Simon & Schuster Speakers Bureau at 1-866-248-3049 or visit our website at www.simonspeakers.com.

Interior design by Kyoko Watanabe

Manufactured in the United States of America

10 9 8 7 6 5 4 3 2 1

The Library of Congress has cataloged the hardcover edition as follows:

Names: Skidelsky, William, author.
Title: Federer and me : a story of obsession / William Skidelsky.
Description: First Atria Hardcover edition. / New York : Atria Books, 2016. /
    "First published in Great Britain in 2015 by Yellow Jersey Press"—T.p. verso.
Identifiers: LCCN 2015034273
Subjects: LCSH: Federer, Roger, 1981– / Tennis players—Switzerland—
    Biography.
Classification: LCC GV994.F43 S56 2016 / DDC 796.342092—dc23 LC
    record available at http://lccn.loc.gov/2015034273

ISBN 978-1-5011-3393-0
ISBN 978-1-5011-3394-7 (pbk)
ISBN 978-1-5011-3395-4 (ebook)

*For my father, Robert, who gave me a love of the game,
and to my wife, Gudrun, who helped me see beyond it.*

CONTENTS

CONTENTS

London, Sunday, July 6, 2014

I wake up late, with a question in my head. Will I be going to the Wimbledon final? Before yesterday, this wasn't something I'd even considered. On Friday, when he won his semi against Milos Raonic (three 6–4 sets: surprisingly straightforward), I was so happy—so *stunned*—that he was in the final that I barely gave a thought to the possibility of my being there. But now I'm desperate to make it if I can. I've watched Federer play live about twenty times over the years, and nine times in just the past month, but I've never seen him play a Grand Slam final. Surely, this is my one opportunity: he'll never make it to another major final, at least not one I have a hope of going to. And if he does win—not likely, admittedly—how great to be able to say: *I was there.* All in all, it has to be done.

But how? Needless to say, I don't have a ticket. Centre Court tickets are notoriously hard to get hold of at the best of times. For the final, they're virtually unobtainable. The usual fallback—queuing—isn't an option; the All England Club doesn't release turnstile tickets from the semis onwards. (For understandable reasons: the queues would be absurd.) Basically, to attend a Wimbledon final, you have to be one of four things: extremely lucky in the public ballot; extremely well connected; extremely rich; a member of the Royal Family. Sadly, none of these applies to me, although my mother did discover that she is distantly related to Camilla Parker-Bowles.

The debentures are, of course, a possibility. And I haven't ruled them out. Most Wimbledon tickets are "strictly non-transferable." In other words, the person who buys them has to be the one who uses them. The club strictly enforces this—or claims to. Debentures are different. Basically, it's a system of seat leasing. You buy a five-year debenture—the current cost for Centre Court debs is £50,000—which entitles you to all the tickets for a particular pair of seats during that period. And these tickets, unlike others, are yours to do what you want with. You can give them to friends; you can sell them on. And the debenture holders often do the latter, raking in tidy sums. A pair of Centre Court debenture tickets for a normal day typically goes for two or three thousand. For the men's final, the figure is up near ten grand. In 2013, when Andy Murray won, there were rumors of pairs of tickets swapping hands for £30,000. In other words, debentures not only enable their holders to see lots of tennis; they can be a smart investment. Making pleasure profitable—an old English talent.

For the last twenty-four hours, I've been keeping tabs on the various websites on which debenture tickets are sold, in the hope that some strange market anomaly will result in one suddenly becoming available at a less-than-stratospheric price. This hasn't happened. The cheapest single ticket I've found is £4,000. I'm still tempted. I happen (unusually for me) to have a bit of cash in the bank. Not a huge amount, but enough to cover the ticket. And I probably would go ahead, were it not for one thing: the thought of having to tell my wife. She is currently away in Suffolk with our two-year-old son. She is eight months pregnant. She is already cross with me because I was supposed to be joining them yesterday, but I postponed on the off chance that I managed to get to the final. If, in addition, she discovers that I've spent four thousand on a ticket—well, I can't imagine her response would be sanguine. "You've done *what*? Spent *how* much? Our savings—our children's future—frittered away on *some fucking tennis match . . .* ?"

No, that avenue is definitely closed. But there is one other option: the touts.

As at all major sporting events, the touts come out in force for Wimbledon. I've often seen them myself, near Southfields Tube station, lurking outside cafés, loitering by advertising hoardings. Mostly, the polished hordes who process up Wimbledon Park Road don't give them so much as a second glance. The tennis-watching public aren't interested in their furtive queries, their wheeler-dealings. ("Got any tickets you want to sell, mate?" "Need to get into Centre Court?")

But there's surely something a bit odd about the touts at Wimbledon. How, after all, can they exist? If, as the All England Club claims, tickets for the tournament are "strictly non-transferable"—if the club really is scrupulous about enforcing this—then there wouldn't be any point in buying touted tickets. They'd be a waste of money. Of course, it could be that the touts only handle debentures. But as the debenture holders have websites they can legitimately trade their tickets on, why would they bother using the touts, who presumably demand a sizable cut? (Or to put it another way: Why would legitimate touts bother selling their tickets through illegitimate ones?) When you think about it, it doesn't quite stack up. In fact, there are only two scenarios that explain the touts' presence. Either they are total scammers, dedicated to ripping off gullible Joe Public by off-loading unusable tickets. Or the Wimbledon authorities aren't as strict about checking the provenance of tickets as they claim.

When, at around 11 a.m., I find myself on the phone to a man named Sam, whose ad for suspiciously cheap finals tickets I spotted on Gumtree, I am still unsure as to which of these two hypotheses is correct. But I am beginning to suspect that I will soon find out. Sam tells me that, yes, he can sort me out a ticket, so long as I can make it to a particular café near Southfields Tube within the hour. The price will be £900. ("Yeah, I would like cash.") Nine hundred pounds is, of course, a lot of money—still far too much, really, to spend on a tennis match. But I also think that, at this three-figure level, there's some vague possibility that my wife will be sympathetic. She does live with me, after all. She knows how *seriously* I take this stuff.

I get dressed, and set off on my scooter. It will take me just under an hour to get to Wimbledon. All I have to do is withdraw the money from a cashpoint on the way. But here I discover a flaw in my plan. My bank only lets me take out £500 per day. To obtain more, customer services tell me, I'll need to visit a branch, which is impossible, it being Sunday. For a few minutes, I am in despair. To get so close and be denied! But then I collect myself. All is not lost. Surely I can borrow the extra from friends. First, though, I ring Sam back to double-check: is there any chance—any chance *at all*—he'd accept a check? He's unyielding: "I'd like to help, mate, but I'm afraid my company doesn't handle checks." In that case, can he hang on for an hour or so? He sounds distinctly dubious.

I hurriedly make phone calls. An ex-flatmate agrees to lend me £150 if I transfer the money into her account the next day. Next I get hold of Jack, who lives a bit farther away but, handily, is a shipping lawyer. He seems positively delighted by my request. "Of course, come on over," he says, as if inviting me to pop round for a drink. I get to his house at noon. He's still in his dressing gown. ("Party last night . . .") I'd assumed that he would have gone to a cashpoint, but evidently this wasn't necessary: yawning, he reaches into one of his pockets and extracts a wad of notes. "Now, are you sure two fifty is enough? Don't you want a little more, just in case . . . ?"

Shortly before one, I arrive at the café with £1,000 in my wallet. I get out my phone, notice that my wife has called. I dial Sam's number. No reply. I try again. Nothing. It rings endlessly. This is, unquestionably, a further blow, but, looking around, I realize that it may not be a fatal one. There are other touts in the vicinity, arranged in small clusters. I position myself near one group, make eye contact. A leather-jacketed man peels off, walks towards me, nods his head across the road—where a pair of policeman are standing—and signals for me to follow him down a side alley. "You want tickets for the final?" is his inevitable opening gambit.

"Well, just the one, please, if you've got any," I reply.

"Hmmm, not sure if we've got any singles rights now, but wait here a minute, I'll check with Dave."

Dave comes over: he's gray-skinned, in his late forties, veiny round the eyes. "You want a single? Think I can get you one. But it won't be a posh seat." We haggle over the price. He wants a thousand; I bring him down to eight fifty. (The day's business is drawing to a close; the touts, I guess, want to off-load their tickets.) Dave now enters into a discussion with the leather-jacketed man, conducted almost entirely in slang: words like "carpet," "stretch," and "nevis" feature prominently. I am led to a café, where I sit down with a third man, whose job, it seems, is to act as my minder. He's pleasant, in a laconic way. After a few minutes, a woman arrives, accompanied by a boy who looks about four years old. She and the minder know each other: "Hello, Steve, how's it going?"

"Not too bad, thanks. Not long to go here. How's the little fella?"

They chat for a while, talk about another man who, it seems, is about to be released from prison. My feelings about the touting fraternity are rapidly becoming warmer. In contrast to their feral depiction in the media, these people, despite their nefarious dealings, appear to belong to a close-knit community.

While my minder and the woman chat, my phone rings. It's my wife. "Where are you?" she says. "Are you going to come down today?"

I explain that I'm not going to make it after all, that I'm in a café near Wimbledon, about to hand over £850 to a tout in exchange for a ticket that should—no, *will*—get me into the final.

"A tout?" she says. "Are you crazy?"

I tell her that I have a good feeling about it, that the guy I'm buying the ticket from seems honest; she replies that I should pull out right away. Then I notice that Steve is beckoning. "Look, sorry, I have to go."

We head to a nearby pub, where Dave is sitting at a table with an Indian-looking man, who's counting out a large sum of money. My ticket, it seems, is a spare from an exchange with a larger group. When he's finished, Dave sits down next to me, hands me my ticket. There's a name on it—Mark Simpson—and a price: £148. It looks real enough. The date is correct. But how can I be certain that it will get me in? What happens, I ask, if they ask me to prove that I am Mark Simpson?

Dave smiles. "Relax. They hardly ever check. But if you're worried, just head round the side, and go in through that gate at the back, number nineteen, is it? The guys there aren't bothered." I still must be looking apprehensive, because Dave adds: "Look, if you have any problems, just come back here and see us." Will he give me my money back? "Yeah, yeah, I will, no problems."

I get out my wallet, start counting my cash. Meanwhile, Dave's on the phone, dispensing more instructions: "Tell him I've got a maggie and a bottle. So I'm going to take a monkey and give back a stretch, then we'll be all-square."

So fastidious is Wimbledon's traditionalism, I reflect, that even the touts are out of an Ealing comedy. I keep my wallet under the table, to avoid detection by any plain-clothed policeman lurking in the vicinity (not that it isn't obvious what we're up to). I'm flustered, though—my hands shake—and I keep miscounting, forcing me to start all over again. Dave breaks off his call: "Jesus, I can make money faster than you can count it." Finally, I assemble the correct amount. Dave scrolls through the bills with practiced ease. The deal is done. We shake hands. I haven't (yet) been arrested.

As I walk up Wimbledon Park Road, my wife calls again. "Look, I think this is a really bad idea. You're wasting an awful lot of . . ."

I butt in, tell her it's too late, that I'm already heading towards the grounds with my ticket. "But it's OK," I say. "The guy said I can get my money back if anything goes wrong."

This information fails to have its intended effect. "A tout says he'll give you a refund and you believe him? Bloody hell, how naïve *are* you?"

I tell her that it's too late to worry about that, I'm about to go in.

And indeed, as it transpires, her fears *are* misplaced. The guy at the gate glances at my ticket, tears the stub, waves me through. I feel the childish thrill of having got away with something, which makes the thought of the £850 I've just spent easier to stomach. I walk the familiar route round the back of Court One, past Henman Hill, thickly crested with people. At the front of the crowd, right in the middle, I spot Tani, whom I met just a few weeks ago in Halle. She may be the most devoted Federer fan I've ever met—in fact, one of the most ardent Federer fans in the entire world—and even she hasn't got a ticket! I wave, but she doesn't see me. I buy an overpriced, underflavored bowl of nachos and make my way to Centre Court.

My seat isn't great: I'm one row from the very back. Because of the way the roof slopes down, there's a strange tunneling effect: it's as if I'm looking on the court through a viewfinder. The atmosphere up here is hemmed in, close; we're in our own little world. But it doesn't matter. Federer is about to play another Wimbledon final, and here *I* am, about to watch it.

chapter one

The sporty one

1.

I first saw him play eleven years before this, in 2003. Also at Wimbledon, also on Centre Court. It wasn't love at first sight.

During the first week of the tournament, I received a call from a friend. He had a spare ticket for next day. Would I like to go? Although I wasn't a big tennis fan back then, it was an offer I felt I couldn't refuse. The only problem was practical. How to get out of work? I'd recently started a job as junior books editor on a weekly current affairs magazine, and the day in question—a Thursday—was our deadline. Moreover, my boss was away, leaving me, for the first time, in sole charge of our section. After giving the matter some thought, I decided that a course of brazenness would be best: I would simply leave—as if heading out for an important meeting. The next day, at noon, I sidled out of our offices, took a Tube to Waterloo, and, from there, caught a train to southwest London. Predictably, my plan was foiled, in the sense that my absence *was* noticed, and resulted in a ticking off. But I've never had any regrets.

It was one of those indecisive early summer days when both sun and rain seem equally plausible. When I got to the All England Club, the first match of the afternoon was already in progress. It was between the fourth seed, Roger Federer, and a left-handed Austrian called Stefan Koubek. I'd heard that Federer, then twenty-one, was an up-and-coming talent, but aside from that I knew nothing about him. My first impression was that, physically, he wasn't terribly prepossessing. He had a ponytail, which, in conjunction with the fat white swathe of his headband, seemed to bring out the squishiness of his features. There was a hint of bum fluff on his upper lip. Despite his all-white attire, he looked like he belonged not on the lawns of SW19 but on the beach—or in some central European heavy metal band. The groomed, chiseled icon hadn't yet emerged from the callow shell of youth.

I arrived near the end of the first set, which Federer won 7–5, saving a set point. The next two sets were much more one-sided: Federer lost a game in each. There was a savagery to his destruction of Koubek, but it was savagery of a particular kind, combining raw power with a delicacy of movement and touch. While his opponent lurched and lumbered, Federer danced around the court in quick, light steps, never seeming to be out of position. His game was virtually soundless, as if the effort cost him nothing. And this impression of calm was reinforced by his demeanor, which was curiously expressionless, almost a blank.

I remember that all this came as a surprise—even a shock—to me. For it wasn't what I'd been expecting. Tennis, which when I was a boy *had* been massively important to me, had faded from my life, partly because of a growing sense that the game was no longer what it had been. Where once matches had involved artistry and guile, now they tended to be contests of strength. On the slick grass of Wimbledon, they would pass in a flurry of booming aces and unreturned serves. On slower courts, they would consist mainly of pounding baseline rallies. Yet here was Federer successfully deploying a different approach, one redolent of an earlier, subtler era. Yes, his game was powerful, but it relied on timing rather than muscle. It had a precision, a sense of craft, that brought to my mind not only the greats of my boyhood—McEnroe, Edberg, Mandlikova, Graf—but also, reaching further back, the figures I'd glimpsed in grainy black-and-white footage, and in the books I'd pored over as a child: Rosewall, Bueno, Gonzales, Laver.

The afternoon's other matches were more in line with my expectations. Venus Williams swatted aside some hapless Belgian. Then came Greg Rusedski versus Andy Roddick, the day's headline contest. Roddick was another young gun of whom much was expected; in America, he was viewed as heir to Pete Sampras and Andre Agassi. And he was certainly more immediately noticeable than Federer, with his whipper-crack serve and air of anxious bustle. But his match with Rusedski—predictably ace-strewn—was boring. I found neither player remotely enticing. The one moment of real drama was a line dispute. On a key point in the third set, with Roddick serving, someone in the crowd yelled "Out!" when one of the American's shots landed near the baseline. Rusedski, thinking the call genuine, stopped playing. The umpire had no option but to hand Roddick the point, but when he did this Rusedski's frustration, which had been building all afternoon—he was down two sets—unleashed itself in a lengthy, foul-mouthed tirade. "I can't do anything if the crowd fucking calls it . . . Replay the point . . . Some wanker in the crowd changes the match and you allow it to happen. Well done! Well done!" The crowd, I remember, mostly responded with jeers and whistles. The ex-Canadian Rusedski may have been "one of us," but it was clear that he would never replace Tim Henman in our affections.

What I took away from the afternoon was the memory of Federer stooping low against the grass, spearing a backhand up the line, and of the contrast between the gentle-seeming lean of his serve and the percussive crack as the ball—once again—whipped into the back fence for an ace. Those images stayed with me as, over the following week and a half, I monitored his progress through the tournament, telling anyone who would listen how good I thought he was.

In Federer's career, Wimbledon 2003 was a hinge moment, the point when his promise finally came to fruition.

With each match, his confidence billowed, as if he were discovering, for the first time, the full reach of his talents. In the fourth round he beat the young American Mardy Fish in four sets. In the quarters he saw off the gangly Dutch eighth seed, Sjeng Schalken, in three. And then, in the semifinals, he raised his game to extravagant heights to crush the player who seemed most likely to impede his progress: Andy Roddick.

I remember watching that match on TV. After a tight first set, which Federer won on a tiebreak after (again) saving a set point, Roddick was swept away in a torrent of balletic volleys and lancing ground strokes. I was amazed by the ease with which Federer neutralized Roddick's serve, whose up-close ferocity I'd observed for myself a week earlier. He always seemed to know where it was heading, and parried it back seemingly with time to spare. His passing shots, too, were lethal. Countless times, Roddick sent the ball to the corner and headed for the net, only to be left stranded by the sort of whipped, short-angled ground stroke that became a Federer trademark. So comprehensively was Roddick outplayed that, not for the last time in his career, he was frequently made to look inept, foolish.

Two days later, Federer faced another big server, the towering Australian Mark Philippoussis, in the final. To no one's great surprise, he won in straight sets. Though I didn't watch the match (I must have had something else on), I remember taking a pleasure in Federer's victory that was, at least in part, egotistical: it proved that my initial reaction had been correct, that my man—my "spot"—really was something special. (This self-congratulatory impulse, I now realize, was pretty absurd: it wasn't as if he was totally unheard of.) Yet immediately after that tournament, my attention drifted away both from tennis and from Federer, and my life resumed its previous course. I went back to the world of editing, of journalism, of building a sense of myself as an adult. For what now strikes me as a strangely long time—roughly three and a half years—I gave little thought to Federer at all.

2.

While tennis didn't mean much to me in 2003, this hadn't always been the case. As a boy, I loved the sport with an all-consuming passion. Between the ages of about five and eleven, it was—by some distance—the most important thing in my life.

I first played it—or a version of it—in the south of France. My parents owned a house in a village called La Garde-Freinet, a treacherous hour's drive from Saint-Tropez. We used to stay there in the holidays, but in 1981, when I was five, we decamped there for a whole year, as my father, a historian, had taken a sabbatical from his university job in order to write the first volume of his biography of the economist John Maynard Keynes. My eight-year-old brother and I attended the local school, where we learned idiosyncratic French (in my case, a tortuously ungrammatical Franglais) and formed tentative friendships with other kids from the village. It was, I think, an unsettling period for us both. My brother, who never had a good relationship with authority as a child, narrowly avoided being expelled, while I was so alarmed by the infant school's unbarricaded row of sit-down toilets that I refused to use them. (On a few occasions, this stance met with predictably dire consequences; eventually, a special concession was granted whereby I alone, of all the children at the school, was allowed to use the staff facility.) Our younger sister was born in December that year—the first home birth in the village, as the local paper noted, for more than half a century.

At the back of our house was a small walled patio, and in this my father devised a game, played with bats and a foam ball, which I suppose was a cross between tennis, squash, and fives. I think the scoring was based on squash, with games the first to nine. We played this endlessly—there wasn't much to do in the village—and it was during this period, according to my father, that I developed the foundations of what would become my most potent weapon (when I was a child anyway): my single-handed backhand. In fact, my father gave me a nickname that reflected this: "Bumbledon of the backhand."

A year or so after we returned to England, my mother started taking me to short tennis classes at our local leisure center in North London. Short tennis—played on a badminton court with a lowered net, plastic rackets, and a foam ball—was then a popular way to introduce children to the sport.[1] Our coach, Bill, was a mustached man of about forty

---

1. It has now been replaced by Mini-Tennis, which is similar, but played on a specially marked-out section of a full-size court.

who bore a striking resemblance to the Canadian snooker player Cliff Thorburn. Bill was a patient teacher, and had a knack for demystifying the game's more abstruse aspects. I particularly remember his method for illustrating the value of spin. From his pocket he would produce a rubber ball, which he would dispatch from his wrist with savage reverse rotation, instructing us to chase after it. Off we would set, but as soon as the ball hit the ground, it would jag violently back towards him. Helplessly, we'd watch it loop back over us and into the safety of Bill's outstretched palm. At which point he would smile and say: "That's why you need spin."

Aided, no doubt, by my head start in France, I took to short tennis and was identified by Bill as having talent. After a few months, I got the chance to put my skill to the test in the Middlesex Short Tennis Championship—an event that took place, oddly enough, at the same leisure center where our weekly classes were held. (Despite its rather lofty-sounding title, I'm not sure how extensive its reach really was.) My father and I entered the parent-and-child doubles, and I entered the under-10s singles. My father and I easily won the doubles, and in the singles I made it through to the final, where my opponent was a stick-thin boy with a handicap: one of his legs was slightly shorter than the other. The match took place in front of what I remember to be a huge crowd (a makeshift grandstand had been erected along one side of the hall) and was a tense, drawn-out affair. My opponent's disability meant that he moved with a limp, but he covered the court with surprising agility, and was particularly good at running round his (weak) backhand and pummeling my own backhand with his (vicious) forehand. This became the pattern of the match: his forehand to my backhand, point after point. Although my single-hander was my best shot, it eventually faltered in the face of this Nadal-like onslaught, and he ended up a narrow victor.

There is a photograph of me after the match, clutching my plastic runner-up trophy, my eyes flecked with tears. It was my first serious taste of defeat on a tennis court, and I still remember the anguish it caused me, the mix of disbelief and desolation. At school the next day I got to stand up in front of the class and show off my trophy, but it was scant consolation. I felt—for a few days at least—empty inside, as if all meaning had drained from my life. Looking back, I can see that, in many ways, it was for the best that I lost. A year or so later, I encountered my conqueror again, this time on a full-sized court. His disability meant that he was never going to be a good tennis player, and I beat him comfortably. Short tennis had been his one shot at glory.

It was during this period that I saw my first live professional tennis. In November 1984, my mother took my brother and me to the semifinals of the Benson and Hedges Championship, a now-defunct tournament held at the Wembley Arena. I can't remember much about the singles, but I do remember a remarkable doubles featuring a sixteen-year-old Boris Becker and his partner, Emilio Sanchez (brother of Arantxa), up against Ivan Lendl and the Ecuadorian left-hander Andrés Gómez. Becker, who'd only turned pro a few months earlier, was at this point unknown, but his performance that night—a combination of coltlike energy and blazing muscularity—was enthralling. He dominated proceedings, outbludgeoning Lendl from the back, chasing down seemingly impossible balls, firing down countless aces and booming smashes. The crowd, I remember, got more and more excited as the match wore on, not just because the tennis was so thrilling, but because what we were witnessing scarcely seemed credible. Who was this blue-eyed wunderkind? How could he be *this* good? Of course, it wasn't long before Becker's gifts gained wider recognition. The following summer, he rematerialized on the grass, and, to my delight, won Queen's (his first title) and then, three weeks later, became, at seventeen years and 227 days, the youngest-ever men's Wimbledon champion.

I had by this point abandoned short tennis, and moved to the full version of the game. Each week, my brother and I would go for a lesson with Bill at our local public courts. My brother was a good player—like me, he had natural hand-eye coordination—but it was becoming clear that he didn't have any real enthusiasm for the sport. From an early age, he had shown signs of being, as my father liked to put it, "an intellectual." He read serious books, and knew about things like architecture, philosophy, and art. Tennis was something he was prepared to play under sufferance, but he basically regarded all sport—with the exception of table tennis—as a waste of time. My father would often say, with a mixture of ruefulness and pride, that my brother could have been the "first intellectual tennis player." Looking back, I realize that those lessons my brother and I had with Bill were the last point in our childhoods when our interests intersected sufficiently to make any kind of shared activity possible. We were rapidly moving in different directions. Our roles had become defined—he was the "intellectual," I was the "sporty one"—and it wasn't until quite a bit later, when we were both teenagers, that we discovered that we had things in common.

It's certainly true that, by the age of eight or nine, I was a tennis nut. Not only did I play as often as I could, tennis had become the focus of my internal life. Inspired by that first, thrilling glimpse of Becker, I became an avid student of the game, scouring newspaper sports sections and devouring books on its history. To this enterprise I applied a scholar's rigor. No detail was too trivial to escape my attention. I could identify the rackets that different ex-pros used. I could recite the scores of three decades' worth of Wimbledon finals. I knew precisely how many titles long-forgotten players like Bill Tilden and Suzanne Lenglen had won, and whom they had beaten to get them. Inevitably, too, my fantasies for my own future revolved around a glittering tennis career. At home, we had a Ping-Pong table, and I would stand beside it for hours on end, knocking a ball back and forth against the wall, constructing elaborate make-believe matches. In these, I would accomplish every manner of astonishing feat— winning Wimbledon aged *sixteen*, racking up more Grand Slams than Laver, spending an entire decade at No 1. In my dreams, my achievements were limitless.

The reality of my tennis career was more prosaic. Based on my success in short tennis, I became a member of the Middlesex Under 10 Squad. This meant that I went off for training sessions at an indoor center in west London. I played a few matches for the county. I also started entering tournaments, with titles like the Paddington Open and the Middlesex County Closed. I would usually get through a few rounds, before coming up against someone better than me. My particular nemesis at this time was a boy named Gary Le Pla, who was not only the best player for his age in Middlesex, but was ranked number one in the whole southeast region. The first time I played him he beat me, humiliatingly, 6–0, 6–0. The next time I got a few games. However, it was clear that Gary Le Pla existed on a different plane from the likes of me. I have occasionally wondered what became of him. Aged ten, he seemed impossibly good, unquestionably destined for future greatness. Yet to judge from the fact that I never heard of him again, he—like the overwhelming majority of tennis prodigies—never made it.

3.

During this period, I adored watching tennis. But my affection was of a particular kind. It was focused more on the game itself—its history, its facts and figures—than on the fortunes of individual players. That's not to say that I didn't have my preferences; some players appealed to me more than others. Lendl, for example, I never warmed to (too abrasive). Nor did I much care for Chris Evert (too bland). I liked Hana Mandlikova (sumptuous ground strokes) and Stefan Edberg (peerless volleys), and also had an entirely predictable soft spot for the dusky Argentine, Gabriela Sabatini, about whom

Clive James would write a notorious poem entitled "Bring Me the Sweat of Gabriela Sabatini." Becker was probably my favorite male player—at least early on, before he started ranting incessantly. But even in his case, I'm not sure I would describe myself as ever being his *fan*. I was happy enough when he won, but his defeats didn't cut me to the quick. When he lost to an unknown Australian named Peter Doohan in the second round at Wimbledon in 1987, prompting his infamous "I didn't lose a war" soliloquy, I don't remember feeling too upset.

Much the same was the case with my favorite female player, Steffi Graf. She came along a year or two after Becker, just as precocious and, astonishingly, even better than him. I loved watching her; there was something mesmerizing about the sight of her long legs gliding around the court. (I had, I'll admit, a mild crush on those legs; to this day I can't understand Clive James's suggestion, in the same poem, that her "thigh muscles when tense / Look interchangeable with those of Boris Becker.") I was also fascinated by her deadly but unconventional forehand—which she struck with the ball almost behind her—and by the fact that she was hardly ever brave enough to use her topspin backhand, except when her opponent came to the net. But once again, there wasn't much emotional connection. I didn't identify with her plight. The whole concept of being a fan—that is, of caring about one player to the exclusion of all others, of seeing them almost as an extension of oneself—was at this point alien to me.

That's not to say that I didn't have some idea of what it entailed, or what its uses might be. At primary school, I discovered that having a "team" was a necessary social tool, a passport to playground acceptability; on my brother's advice, I became a Liverpool fan, not that I really knew anything about them or even where Liverpool was. And then there was the example of my father, who, throughout my childhood, carried a torch for the American left-hander Jimmy Connors. Quite where this affection came from I never discovered; I don't think even he could account for it. But I remember very clearly the strength of his loyalty, the way it shaped his entire relationship with the sport. At breakfast, he would scour the sports pages of the *Times*, looking for the results section, with its news of far-flung tournaments. He would read out the match scores, pretending to find them all equally interesting. But I knew this even-handedness to be something of a pretense. In reality, he was only interested in one thing: how Connors had done. When he watched Connors on TV, my father's whole demeanor changed. He would become clenched and agitated, visibly on edge. After Connors hit each shot, his shoulders would involuntarily jerk upwards, as if, by this action, he could force the ball over the net. (Connors, famously, hit his shots unusually flat, so to be fair to my father, the risk of him netting them was higher than average.) And even as his career stretched into his thirties, and suffered the inevitable decline, my father remained steadfastly loyal. He carried on believing, against all the evidence, that one day Connors would triumph again.

I remember finding this devotion puzzling. There was nothing particularly likable about Connors. He was an ungainly stylist—though undeniably effective—and, off court, he was known to be a jerk. In fact I remember my father once referring to him—scandalously—as a "typical American shit." It was odd to think that, of all the players my father could have chosen, he'd singled out Connors. Had the decision been purely random? Or did it reveal something about my father? Connors's chief virtue as a player was his doggedness. Was it this that my father admired? That didn't fit with what I knew about his previous sporting enthusiasms; in the past, he'd tended to favor natural stylists like Maria Bueno and the England cricketer Denis Compton. Even as a child, I could see that there was something unfathomable about the whole business of being a fan. In its self-evident irrationality—its blatant disproportionality—it pointed to a mind-set I didn't yet understand.

4.

In 1986, when I was ten, my life underwent a second up-heaval. We left London and moved into John Maynard Keynes's old house in East Sussex. My father took up residence in his subject's former study—which was separated from the main house by a covered walkway—and devoted himself to the task of writing the second (and, subsequently, third) volume of his biography. At first, I persisted with my tennis career. I joined a club in Lewes and again became part of the county set-up. I regularly entered tournaments. But in truth, it was around this time that the intensity began to bleach out of my enthusiasm.

The irony was that I now had more opportunities to play than ever before. Our new house had a large garden, and a few months after we moved in my father hired a firm to bulldoze a section of long grass off to the side of the main lawn. Within what seemed like weeks, a gleaming hard court had appeared. Of course, I should have been thrilled by this development, which was undertaken partly for my benefit. And I do remember feeling excited at first. But it wasn't long before other feelings took over. At the secondary school I now attended—as well as at my tennis club—the court was more a source of embarrassment than pride; I had, by this point, acquired an intense fear of being labeled "posh." Meanwhile, at home, its existence underscored the fact that tennis wasn't something that belonged exclusively to me. For reasons that I can't now easily account for, this seemed extremely important. It had to do, I think, with my growing sense of being an outsider at home. We were an academic, intellectual family. It felt like there was a pressure, emanating from my father, to display copious brainpower—to be "intellectual"—at all times. My sportiness, I came to believe, was a badge of inferiority, something that marked me out as insufficiently serious. As a defensive reaction to this growing sense of inadequacy, I cleaved ever more tightly to my sporting identity. Sport had gone from being a boyish passion to becoming my refuge, my escape. I wanted to keep it as separate as possible.

In any case, I had by this point acquired a new obsession. I'd begun watching cricket during the Ashes series of 1985 in the company of a family friend. As well as acquainting me with its elaborate rules and comically arcane terminology ("silly mid-off," "leg glance," "maiden"), he set me straight on such perplexing matters as why, at times, the batsmen seemed to hit constant boundaries, while at others they blocked every ball. It was the difference, he explained, between watching the highlights and watching live Test coverage. Its mysteries elucidated, cricket proved riveting. That summer, once the excitement of Becker's Wimbledon triumph had subsided, I watched, captivated, as England, led by their languid captain David Gower, fought their way to an unexpected 3–1 victory over Alan Border's Australians.

While we lived in London, there had been few opportunities to play cricket. But now, in the country, I joined a local village team. I discovered that I was a good batsman, strong off my legs, and the possessor of a useful square cut, though thoroughly inept as a bowler. Cricket became the second love of my life. Quite how my mother put up with this I don't know as it meant that, in addition to ferrying me to my tennis commitments, she had to act as my cricketing chauffeur. My father, whose labors on Keynes occupied him almost all the time when he was at home, wasn't much help in this regard.

Although I played the two sports in tandem to begin with, cricket soon got the upper hand. As I saw it then, it had a number of advantages over tennis. For one thing, unlike tennis, it *did* feel like my own discovery: no one else in my family had ever played it, aside from my father, briefly, at school. I was also becoming disillusioned with the culture of tennis. At the club, and between matches at tournaments, there was an awful lot of hanging around, and I increasingly found that I didn't have much in common with my fellow players. They seemed simultaneously rooted in the world of tennis, with its clubhouse tedium, its slot-machine banter, and oddly indifferent to the things about the game—its history, the mechanics of Graf's forehand—that I found interesting.

The intensity of the competition was also off-putting. Often, in matches, you'd find yourself having to deal with an opponent far more determined and obstreperous than the one facing you across the net—namely, the parent at the court's edge. You'd have to tune out the hectoring commentary ("You know that's not the way to hit your backhand! Come on!") and the semi-illegal interventions over line calls ("There's no way that shot was out! Go on, claim the point!") My mother also hated this aspect of the sport, and she tells me now that she usually spent my matches reading in the car. Cricket, by contrast, was a more laid-back, less stridently partisan, affair. Parents watched from the boundary, but never intervened. The game's team nature diluted the importance of outcome: as a player, you could excel individually even if your side lost. The teams I played for tended to be run by men who weren't primarily seeking to advance their own children. Many, in fact, were childless. They gave up their evenings and weekends out of simple love for the game.

And so I drifted away from the individualistic world of tennis into the calmer, more collaborative waters of cricket. By the age of thirteen or fourteen, I had more or less abandoned my first sporting love.

My father, it must be said, didn't entirely welcome this development. Aside from anything else, he wanted someone to do battle with on our court at home. Besides me, he only had one regular opponent: our landlord, an eccentric viscount who would turn up to play decked out in Green Flash trainers, flannel trousers, a collared shirt, and, quite often, a tie and jacket as well. His serve was an ornate whirl of arms and racket that struck me as the product of some venerable—possibly nineteenth-century—school of coaching. He had an odd insistence on ensuring that all the balls were off the ground—in either hand or pocket—before a point could commence. He wasn't a bad player, but his style was too lackadaisical to render him effective against my father, who had a pugnacious, if somewhat inconsistent, game. My father's preference for playing me was understandable, given that, from when I was about twelve, we were fairly evenly matched. (He remembers that he beat me more often than I him; oddly enough, I remember the opposite.) Yet increasingly, I turned down his requests for games, citing schoolwork or cricket-related fatigue. In tennis matters, I became sullen and uncooperative. And so, gradually, our court fell into disuse. Cracks appeared in the surface, from which weeds began to protrude. A tide of moss crept in from the fence on one side, eventually swallowing up most of a tramline. Occasionally my mother would put down weed killer, but this did little to halt the damage. Nature's work of reclamation was irreversible.

Around this time, I also lost much of my appetite for watching the sport. Tennis in the nineties struck me as a soulless affair, lacking the color and diversity it had displayed in the eighties. Maybe I felt this simply because I was older, and less infatuated with the sport generally, but I also think a genuine change took place. At some point towards the end of the eighties, tennis shed its adolescent exuberance and became more straitlaced and serious. Earlier in the decade, a certain wildness had pertained, a sense of theatricality and excess: Becker flinging himself around on the grass; Pat Cash clambering into the crowd after his 1987 Wimbledon triumph; McEnroe throwing his epic tantrums. The game still had a touch of seventies glamour. Now that spirit vanished, or at least receded. The players no longer appeared to care how much entertainment they were providing. Many of the new breed—Jim Courier, Michael Chang, Thomas Muster, and, on the women's side, Monica Seles—struck me as thoroughly, blandly professional, machinelike in their relentlessness. They were no match, in terms of personality or style, for the likes of Edberg and Becker, Graf and Mandlikova. Technically, too, they were all depressingly similar. (Seles, with her two-fisted ground strokes on both wings, was an exception, but her uniqueness didn't strike me as a good thing.)

In fact, there was only one player whom I consistently enjoyed watching during this period: Pete Sampras. Although his personality was bland and he had an unfortunate habit of sticking his tongue out between points, he was, especially on the grass at Wimbledon, a majestic player to behold, with his arch-backed serve (surely the best of all time) and superlative command at the net. Not only was he outstandingly good, but his playing style, with its lazy grandeur, seemed to place him at odds with his era. His game struck me as having a classical stamp to it. Yet even he couldn't rekindle my passion.

Tennis had by this point lost most of its magic, and I doubted I'd ever love it again.

5.

As I said, it took me a while to become obsessed with Federer. In the years following my first sighting of him at Wimbledon, I paid him relatively little attention. I kept vague tabs on his results but I didn't watch many of his matches. The problem was that I had too much else going on. I was in my midtwenties and was trying to carve out a niche for myself in the adult world—a goal that, since university, had seemed impossibly distant. Work preoccupied me a good deal: I was finally making some headway as a journalist. There were the standard midtwenties social pursuits: going to parties, hanging out with friends. And I was falling in love—something that hadn't happened in quite a while. My relationship with my new girlfriend—a fellow journalist—was all-consuming. The result was that Roger Federer, for all his appeal, seemed like a distant, tangential figure. My life didn't have room in it for me to become obsessed with him.

By late 2006, though, things were beginning to change. I had just turned thirty and I felt less pressured at work. My relationship was running into trouble; my girlfriend and I hadn't split up, but it increasingly seemed like a possibility. We were spending less time together (or rather, she was spending less time with me) and this meant, among other things, that I had more time on my hands. I'd also recently started playing tennis again. Through work, I'd met various writers and publishers who were enthusiastic players. The great thing about writers is that they tend to be available to play at any time, unbeholden as they are to office timetables. This suited me. Although I had a desk job, I found that there were plenty of opportunities to bunk off and play tennis: I could nip out at lunchtime, or arrange early-morning hits. (Journalists, in my experience, aren't generally expected to be at their desks before ten a.m.) Although rusty to begin with—I'd barely picked up a racket in fifteen years—I soon located the remnants of my game and some of my former fluency returned. To my surprise, I not only discovered that I loved playing, but that I was a match for the cream of London's tennis-playing literati.

Playing a sport, of course, isn't a prerequisite for becoming a fan. But it does help. As a consequence of taking up tennis again, I became more susceptible to the allure of Federer. I started paying closer attention to his results and I couldn't help but notice how phenomenally successful he was being. Whole years seemed to go by in which he would barely lose a match. In the summer of 2006, at a family gathering of my girlfriend's, I remember meeting an aspiring tennis pro, a young British player on the fringes of the tour. I asked him whom, of today's top players, he particularly admired. He told me he'd recently been on some practice courts near Federer and he couldn't believe how good he was. As he spoke, awe entered his voice and his eyes acquired a faraway look. Increasingly, I realized, this was how Federer was being viewed. He was becoming a figure of legend, almost a god.

Not long after this, I happened to stumble across an essay on Federer by David Foster Wallace. It was first published in the *New York Times*, but I read a reprint in the *Guardian*. I was already a fan of Wallace's writing—his fiction in particular—and the piece, unsurprisingly, made a big impression on me. Here was a palpably clever writer—something of a genius himself—talking in candidly reverential terms about the wonder, the *beauty*, of Federer's tennis. I was struck not only by Wallace's concept of the "Federer moment"—the instances when his play appears to defy the laws of physics—but also by the way he sought to locate his subject within the game's overall trajectory. His argument had a density, a subtlety, to it that I had rarely encountered in sports writing. And his sense of the sport's development very much chimed with my own.

Wallace's basic contention was that men's tennis had, for the previous few decades, been moving in a linear direction. Thanks to a combination of composite rackets, related changes in technique, and advances in athleticism, a single style had come to dominate the sport. This style—the "power baseline" game—was, as its name suggested, based on hitting the ball with tremendous power (and copious topspin) from the back of the court. According to Wallace, it was Lendl who had pioneered the style in the eighties, in the nineties players like Agassi and Courier had raised it to new heights, and, more recently, Rafa Nadal had taken it "just as far as it goes." The problem with the power baseline style, Wallace suggested, wasn't that it was inherently boring—it was actually an improvement on the "two-second points of old-time serve and volley or the moon-ball tedium of classic baseline attrition"—but it was "somewhat static and limited" and, if it were to prove the "evolutionary end-point of tennis," that would be a problem for the game.

Federer, however, had shown another way forward. He had introduced—or rather, reintroduced—elements such as subtlety and variety, an "ability to read and manipulate opponents, to mix spins and speeds, to misdirect and surprise, to use tactical foresight and peripheral vision." Yet the point about Federer—and here was Wallace's kicker—was that he could do all those things while *also* being a "first-rate, kick-ass power baseliner." He had demonstrated a new way of playing tennis that was as attractive as it was effective, and had done so from *within* the modern game. "With Federer, it's not either/or," Wallace wrote. "The Swiss has every bit of Lendl or Agassi's pace on his groundstrokes, and leaves the ground when he swings, and can out-hit even Nadal from the backcourt . . . It's just that that's not all he [has] . . . He is Mozart and Metallica and the combination is somehow wonderful."

Wallace ended his essay on a note of optimism. At that year's Wimbledon, which he'd attended, the junior event had been a "variegated ballet," with players deploying "drop volleys and mixed spins, off-speed serves, gambits planned three shots ahead—all as well as the standard-issue grunts and booming balls." The clear implication was that Federer's approach was starting to influence tennis more widely, expanding the sport's very possibilities. "For the first time in years," Wallace wrote, "the game's future is unpredictable."

6.

Every line of Wallace's analysis intrigued me and his words were still in my head a month or so later when, in Shanghai, I chanced upon Federer on TV. My brother was living in the city for a semester, teaching the history of Western political theory at one of its universities. In November, I went to stay with him for a week. For the first few days of my visit, my brother had teaching duties, and so while he went out to school Shanghai's youth in the benefits of democracy, I mooched around his apartment. The Tennis Masters Cup— the end-of-year tournament featuring the world's top eight players, which at that point was held in Shanghai—was on; there were posters advertising it all over the city.

Switching on the telly one afternoon, I happened upon Federer, again playing Roddick. Through the haze of my jetlag, I watched, transfixed. Roddick was playing well and for most of the first two sets appeared the more likely winner. But then, just when things were beginning to look desperate for Federer, he upped his game. Shots that had been winning Roddick the point not only started coming back, but started coming back as winners. Angles that had previously seemed closed to Federer suddenly became available. This went on for half an hour or so, a period during which Federer appeared incapable of missing—responded, indeed, to each successive difficulty by coming up with an even more spectacular shot. The momentum swung decisively and Federer comfortably won the third set.

I watched with a rising sense of astonishment. I already knew—or thought I knew—how good Federer was, but this was brilliance beyond anything I'd imagined. I remember leaping up off the sofa, dancing with joy, my exclamations mingling with the utterances of the Chinese commentators. Perhaps it was the result of my discombobulated condition— the jet lag, the unfamiliar surroundings—but Federer's tennis that afternoon struck me as unearthly, stupendous, possessed of a magnificence I'd never before seen on a tennis court. I hadn't known such excellence was possible. And the effect upon me was instantaneous. By the time the match was over, something in me had begun to shift. My future—or a part of it—had been determined. I knew that I wanted to follow this man, take what opportunities I could to luxuriate in the silky wondrousness of his play.

My obsession had begun.

2007–2010

Did I choose to become a Federer fan, or was the process involuntary? Although it's more romantic to depict myself as having no real say in the matter, there was a time, early on, when I think things could have gone either way. In this regard, becoming a fan is like falling in love: before the headlong plunge, there's often a period of indeterminacy, when the outlines of the thing you're feeling—this new fascination—remain unclear. At this stage, you're still a free agent: you can draw back or push on, cling to your independence or submit. Opt for the latter, and you'll soon relinquish all decision-making capability, but until that happens, a degree of agency is involved.

For the first year or so after my Shanghai revelation, this was how things were with Federer. I'd been enchanted, bewitched by his brilliance, but I hadn't yet been utterly ensnared. My affection still had an unlodged quality. One indication of this is that I didn't yet feel the need to watch every one of his matches. Lacking satellite TV (though I'd acquire it soon enough) and the ability to stream his matches (did live streaming even exist in those days?), my Federer viewing remained fitful, opportunistic.

For him, 2007 was a year of transition. He entered it in one phase of his career and left it in another. Total supremacy gave way not to decline exactly, but to something less otherworldly. Federer's truly great years—when his tennis really did seem flawless—were 2004–2006. During those seasons, he played a total of 262 matches and lost just fifteen: a win–loss ratio of more than 94 percent. He won thirty-four tournaments and eight Grand Slams. Dominance on this scale, even in a single season, is exceptionally rare in men's tennis. For it to have happened three years in a row was unprecedented.[2]

By any normal standards, 2007 was also extremely good. Overall, Federer won 88.3 percent of his matches and claimed eight titles. He reached the finals of all four Grand Slams, winning three. At the Australian Open he didn't lose a single set. (The previous male player to win a Grand Slam without dropping a set had been Bjorn Borg, in 1980.) He capped the year by winning the Tennis Masters Cup. But

---

2. There is a counterargument to the view that this was a remarkable achievement, which is that the competition during this period wasn't particularly fierce. Nadal was still very young; Djokovic and Murray were barely on the scene; Federer's main rivals were the likes of Hewitt, Safin, and an ageing Agassi. All this is true, but it's not as if those players were walkovers, and in any case, the apparent feebleness of the field is largely a product of viewing it from the perspective of the current era, when the men's game is exceptionally strong. Most epochs don't have a "big four"; many don't even have a "big two."

there were more losses than usual, including a few unfathomable ones: twice, in consecutive tournaments in the spring, he was beaten by the little-known Argentinian Guillermo Cañas; then, on the clay in Rome, he lost to Filippo Volandri, an Italian ranked fifty-three in the world. Were these the first signs that his stranglehold was slipping?

The match I have the clearest memory of that year, unsurprisingly, is the Wimbledon final—his second in succession against Nadal. In 2006, Federer won in four sets; this time it went to five. The match, I now realize, was another milestone in my fanship: it was the first time I remember seriously caring about the outcome. Previously, when I'd watched Federer, the experience had never felt particularly fraught. I had simply relished the spectacle of his superiority. But this time it was different. Federer appeared vulnerable, genuinely threatened. Halfway through the match I realized how very sad I would be if he lost. This feeling—which I suppose was a sign that I was moving into a new, more invested phase of my fanship—caught me unawares. When he hit that famous inside-in forehand to break Nadal in the final set, I remember rising to my feet and punching the air, and being surprised to find myself acting in such a manner.

The following year, the chinks of vulnerability became more glaring still. Federer's overall performance markedly declined. He won just four titles in 2008, and his win–loss ratio slid to 81.5 per cent, its lowest since 2002 (and the lowest it would be until the *annus horribilis* of 2013). This was the year, I think, when the phrase "the old Federer" started being used. It was clear that something significant was happening, that the years of plenty were over. I have memories from this period of regularly seeing Federer's forehand—previously so trusty, so invulnerable—suddenly going off midway through a match. It barely seemed believable. Physical factors played a part: in March, Federer revealed that he had been diagnosed with glandular fever. He nonetheless went on to reach the Wimbledon final (which he came agonizingly close to winning) and then, in September, won his fifth consecutive US Open, beating Andy Murray in the final. But the statistics were unarguable: his success was diminishing.

That summer, not long after Federer's despair-inducing loss to Nadal at Wimbledon, I moved into a new flat in South London, and treated myself to a Sky TV "multi-room package." (I had a new job at a Sunday paper and, for the first time ever, felt reasonably well off.) My parents had recently given me a present of a massive flat-screen TV, which they'd found too imposing for their own sitting room. This I now installed in my bedroom. It was perfect: when Federer was playing in far-off places, at inconvenient hours of the night, I could watch him without even having to rise from my bed. Set the alarm, reach for the remote control, and hey presto: there he was!

It's probably not a coincidence that 2008 was the year my obsession ratcheted up a notch, became wholly entrenched within me. For me, this was a period of emotional turmoil. The girlfriend I'd acquired a few years earlier had ended our relationship in 2007. I took this very hard. Shortly afterwards, I got together with the woman who would become my wife. But not enough time had elapsed since the previous relationship had ended, and I wasn't yet ready for a new one.

I couldn't commit. Throughout 2008 and 2009, I behaved idiotically; my new girlfriend and I split up—and then reunited—several times. I tested her patience to its limits.

Looking back, I can see that, during this confused time, Federer functioned as a point of constancy, of stability. It was as if he provided the security I craved but couldn't achieve. There was a comfort in knowing that, throughout the year, he would be playing somewhere, and wherever that was, I could tune in and watch. And I'm sure it was significant, too, that his career was already in decline, that he was losing his aura of invulnerability. The losses he suffered—and there were some truly crushing ones—produced a pain that resonated within me, and the effect, paradoxically, was oddly consoling.

These years, of course, weren't all bad for Federer. He remained, with Nadal, one of the two best players in the world. And he had some great wins: the 2008 US Open; his first (and only) French Open the following summer; the 2010 Australian Open. Yet glorious as such moments were, it was the losses that seemed significant, that made the biggest mark.

In 2010, my own period of emotional turbulence came to an end. I don't know what exactly caused the change, but I suddenly realized that I was in danger of throwing away the opportunity I had—the best opportunity I ever would have—to make a life with the beautiful, strong, intelligent woman I loved. Just in time, I veered away from the train-wreck course I'd been stuck on. My girlfriend took some convincing that I was serious, but eventually I managed to persuade her. I'm so grateful that this happened, and for how everything has turned out.

chapter two

Federer and the modern game

1.

Tennis has changed a great deal over the last four decades, arguably more than any other major sport. This transformation has taken an unusual form: while the game's rules have remained static (give or take a few minor tweaks, such as the introduction of tiebreaks in the early seventies), its character has altered almost beyond recognition. The most obvious difference is that it has dramatically speeded up. Players hit the ball much harder than they once did and, partly because of this, move around the court faster. In general, today's players are much more athletic than their predecessors: stronger, taller, more explosive and indefatigable. The method they use to hit the ball—technique—has also evolved. The modern forehand, a shot purpose-built to load the ball with immense power and topspin, is mechanically—and aesthetically—very different from the side-on, "classic" stroke of earlier eras. On the backhand side, an overwhelming majority of players today use the double-hander, whereas before the late 1980s it was relatively unusual (and before the 1960s, virtually unknown).

Thirdly, there's strategy. Part of the reason tennis is compelling is that it offers so much scope for tactical variation. Decisions—of many different types—constantly have to be made. In the past, the most fundamental of these related to court position. Unlike, say, in badminton or table tennis, tennis players have the option whether or not to let the ball bounce. They can construct rallies from or behind the baseline, or from the net, and within an individual rally they can switch between the two. Playing at the net dramatically changes a player's risk–reward ratio: volleys are riskier than ground strokes, but also (assuming they go in) much more effective, because they take time away from the opponent and give access to sharper angles.

Throughout much of the sport's history, there was a basic equality between baseline and forecourt. A skillful volleyer could compete on level terms with a strong baseliner; it wasn't clear that one method was superior (although the balance shifted depending on surface: on slow courts, baseliners tended to dominate, on fast courts, volleyers had the upper hand). Yet this is no longer the case. In recent decades, there has been a huge, quite unprecedented swing towards the baseline—and this has occurred across all surfaces, and in both the men's and women's games. The result is that net play has become much less common and what was historically the sport's most important strategic variation has significantly retreated, if not quite disappeared.

2.

There is no great mystery as to what the major cause of these changes has been. Modern tennis is the offspring of technology. By far the most important technological development to affect tennis occurred around the start of the 1980s, when large-headed rackets constructed from carbon-fiber composite, or "graphite," replaced both the wooden ones that had always existed and the steel or aluminium ones that some players had been using since the late sixties. Although their true significance wasn't apparent right away, graphite rackets ultimately transformed the sport, making possible the powerful, highly physical playing style that is the norm today. (A second significant, although less disruptive, shift occurred in the late 1990s and early 2000s, with the emergence of a new generation of artificial—i.e., nongut—strings known as co-polys; these intensified the effects of the earlier revolution by further increasing the amount of spin players could impart to the ball.)

Although there is no doubt as to the overall pattern of modern tennis—graphite rackets led to more power and spin, making the game as it's now played possible—there are several aspects of the story that are not well understood, or open to differing interpretations. For example, what *exactly* was it about the new rackets that led the sport to become so much more powerful? The answer is more complex than many people assume (i.e., it wasn't simply a case of the new rackets being more powerful than the old ones). Then there are other, related, mysteries. For example, why has the single-handed backhand largely vanished from the sport (notwithstanding recent signs that, at least on the men's side, it is reviving)? Ditto serve and volleying: Why, having been such a prominent features of men's (if no longer women's) tennis in the nineties, did it so abruptly disappear in the early 2000s? These developments clearly have something to do with changes to racket technology. But what exactly?

Finally, there is the big evaluative question: Have the changes of recent decades been good or bad? Have they made tennis more or less enjoyable to watch? On this, opinions markedly differ. Some commentators (among them John McEnroe) have argued that graphite rackets were the worst thing that ever happened to tennis; others have claimed that they saved it.[1] Part of the problem in forming a judgment is that a specific change can have many, and often unforeseen, consequences. While the advent of a new technology may at first entail A, later on, it may entail B, C, and D as well. At the same time, there is more than one criterion by which sport can be judged. The pleasures of spectatorship are multifarious. Person X may value one thing, person Y another—and in

1. See, for example, "Spin Doctors" by Tom Perrotta, *The Atlantic*, July 1, 2006.

any case, these priorities may shift over the generations, and may themselves be influenced by the sport's development. For example, as tennis becomes more physically powerful, power may be something that spectators come to value more than in the past. In other words, trying to arrive at a straightforward "good" or "bad" verdict is all but impossible.

3.

To a tennis nerd like myself, questions of this kind—to do with how the sport has interacted with technology—are fascinating in their own right. But they also directly bear on Federer. As the ex-cricketer Ed Smith pointed out,[2] great athletes often give the impression of straddling different eras, of "retaining a link with tradition while anticipating the future." And this is certainly true of the Swiss. Others describe him—in a not dissimilar vein—as a "throwback." But what would be most accurate, I think, is to say that his tennis engenders a certain feeling of timelessness. When you watch him, there's a sense that the sport's history is opening up before you, that you are gaining access not just to its present but also to its past. One way to think of Federer is as a palimpsest—a text on which the various stages of tennis's development have been successively inscribed.

This is not the case with other players. Players like Nadal and Djokovic, for example, are emphatically contemporary,

2. "The Last Days of Roger Federer," *New Statesman,* October 21, 2013.

unburdened by the sport's rich history. Or, to put it another way, their styles—and overall approaches—are rooted in the technological changes of recent decades. There is nothing old school, nothing pregraphite, about them.[3] The point about Federer is not that his game isn't dependent on modern technology: he would be incapable of doing many of the things he does if he played with a wooden racket. But his game isn't *limited* to what technology has made possible. Various aspects, from the way he moves to the basic appearance of his shots, look—indeed in many ways are—premodern.

All this could be taken as suggesting that Federer is an essentially conservative figure, while someone like Nadal is more radical and progressive. After all, throwing off tradition can be an act of boldness. When, many years ago, I interviewed the Catalan chef Ferran Adrià of El Bulli fame, I was struck by the vehemence of his anti-traditionalism.[4] He saw it as his mission to revolutionize cooking, and the way to do this, he said, was to reject all that had gone before, to throw out the rule book

---

3. In Nadal's case, "hyper-contemporary" might be even more apt: so cut off does his style seem from the sport's past that it's positively futuristic.

4. El Bulli, situated on the coast two hours north of Barcelona, was for more than a decade, until its closure in 2011, widely regarded as the best restaurant in the world. Adrià was the chief pioneer of the style of cooking known as molecular gastronomy (although he himself preferred the term "deconstructivist"), which sought to transform cooking through the adoption of new scientific techniques and unfamiliar ingredients. Meals at El Bulli consisted of a set menu of at least twenty courses. The menus changed completely every year. When I went, in 2000, Adrià was especially keen on reinterpreting Italian staples: there was polenta made from ice cream, spaghetti made from chicken stock, and ravioli made from squid. It remains, by some distance, the most remarkable meal I've ever eaten.

(or rather, the recipe book) and start from scratch. In culinary terms, he was about as radical as anyone can be.

Yet whether something is radical or not also depends on the context. Adrià was reacting against—as he saw it—centuries of stifling traditionalism, an insistence that everything had to be done according to a narrow, unbreakable set of rules. And a large part of his radicalism involved using technology in disruptive ways—making polenta, for example, with a faulty ice-cream machine. But the context of tennis is very different. One way it differs is that technology—in the form of graphite rackets—already *had* its disruptive impact. They established—relatively quickly—a new set of orthodoxies; they uprooted the sport from its past. In such circumstances, the relationship between radicalism and traditionalism becomes ambiguous. It could be that what's truly radical isn't to reject tradition but to reconnect with it, to find a new use for old styles and techniques.

This is precisely what Federer has done. What's odd about the Swiss is that he simultaneously resembles lots of other players and no one. His game contains a multitude of stylistic overtones, of grace notes, many harking back to the pregraphite era. And yet no one has ever played tennis remotely like him. His game is both archetypal and unique, rooted in history and seemingly untethered from it.[5] And this, I believe, is the real key to his significance.

---

5. Nadal, on the other hand, is a one-off in a more straightforward way. The American tennis writer L. Jon Wertheim observed, in his book *Strokes of Genius: Federer v. Nadal, Rivals in Greatness*, that one of the striking things about the Spaniard is that his game can't really be compared to anyone else's, past or

4.

By 1976, when I was born, metal rackets had been around for a while. The first one to achieve wide popularity—the Wilson T2000—was launched in 1967, although an earlier incarnation of the same model, made by Lacoste, had been available in Europe since 1963.[6] Broadly following the contours of a wooden racket, but with a throat forged from two steel prongs that started widening just below the head, and with wire hoops inside the frame through which the strings were wound, the T2000 was the racket that the twelve-year-old Jimmy Connors began playing with in the midsixties after receiving a set of prototypes from Wilson. Connors recalls in his autobiography, *The Outsider*, that the first time he hit a shot with it, it "felt like an electric shock" and the ball flew "a mile over the back fence." It took him four or five months to get used to it, during which time he lost virtually every match. But eventually he learned how to harness its unique properties. Because of the T2000's open throat, there was less wind resistance and so he could swing it faster and generate more power. He found he could hit shots that had been "impossible before." And, just as important, he liked the way it

present. For this reason, there isn't anything remotely evocative, or archetypal, about it. Nadal is forward-facing: it's as if he's arrived from the future. Federer is backward-facing: both his game and personality are heavily inflected by the past, yet he manages to seem contemporary too.

6. Actually, the first metal-headed rackets dated back much earlier, to the late nineteenth century, but none had ever taken off.

looked: "silver and modern, different from the rest." It suited Connors to be different.

The T2000 may have been more maneuverable and powerful than its wooden counterparts, but it was also notoriously tricky to play with. Its sweet spot—the area in the center of the string bed that gives access to the most power—was tiny and most players found that it didn't offer good enough control. Although Billie Jean King won the US Open with it in 1967, making her the first player to win a Grand Slam using a nonwooden racket, it didn't ultimately prove a hit with the game's elite. King herself soon reverted to a wooden frame, and during the seventies Connors was the only high-ranked pro to consistently wield the T2000. Undoubtedly, the racket helped him early in his career—the power he could generate with it surprised opponents—but the consensus is that his tardiness in abandoning it (it wasn't until the mideighties that he finally did so) proved a considerable handicap later on.

The T2000 was soon joined by other metal frames, including the Spalding Smasher (with which a forty-one-year-old Pancho Gonzales played his epic match against Charlie Pasarell in the first round at Wimbledon in 1969), the PDP Open (used by the big-serving Roscoe Tanner), and the Head Professional (my father's choice when I was young. I remember very well its thick leather handle and red plastic "bridge" at the base of its head). These first-generation metal rackets—initially made from steel and then more commonly from aluminum—all looked pretty much alike, with their tiny heads, silver bodies, and double-pronged throats.

In 1977 came the next big breakthrough: the appearance

of the first commercially successful oversized frame. (A company called Weed had launched one a year earlier, but it never took off.) The Prince Classic was designed by Howard Head, who'd founded the Head Ski Company where he'd pioneered the development of laminated skis, but was now working for Prince.[7] The Prince Classic had a head size of around 100 square inches—more than 50 percent bigger than the hitherto standard 65 square inches.

Enlarging the head was a logical step, and in fact it had first been attempted as far back as the 1930s. But it only became practical once the viability of non-wooden materials was established. The problem with wood was that it was too weak to support a large head: anything bigger than 65 square inches and the pressure created by having strings tightly wound through it, as well as the ball repeatedly striking it, caused the frame to warp. Before the early eighties, there were no restrictions either on the size of rackets or what materials they could be made of.[8] In a sense, none had ever been necessary, because the dimensions of rackets—27 inches long and 9 inches wide—had always been a function of the stress

7. Confusingly, the Head company, which Howard Head had sold in 1969, was by this point also a major player in tennis rackets, though not yet big-headed ones.

8. The first-ever rule governing racket design, introduced in 1978, concerned strings; its purpose was to outlaw the double-layered, "spaghetti" strings that had appeared a year earlier, and which gave players access to massive spin. The first rule relating to racket shape was introduced in 1981: it set a limit on head size and overall length. Today, rackets are allowed to be 29 inches long and 12.5 inches wide. There have never been any restrictions on material, although there are rules in place that would effectively outlaw any kind of computer-aided racket.

limits of wood. But with tougher materials at their disposal, designers suddenly had the opportunity to experiment.

From a playing point of view, the benefits of large-headed rackets were initially seen as being two-fold: oversized rackets have larger sweet spots, making it easier to time the ball, and they tend to be more powerful, because the enlarged racket face means that the strings bend back further, creating more of a "trampoline effect."

These characteristics made oversized frames particularly attractive to amateurs. For players of a modest standard, one of the biggest challenges of tennis is simply to hit the ball in the right place on the racket. The larger the sweet spot, the easier this is. Equally, weaker (and especially older) players tend not to have the technique or strength to generate that much power themselves, and so a larger, and hence more powerful, head is a help. Yet these qualities mattered less to professionals. Good players can consistently find the sweet spot even with a small-headed racket, and nor do they necessarily need a powerful frame, since they can supply the required power themselves. What advanced players value most in a racket is control, and it's in this area that the early large-headed rackets fell short.

The fault lay with the material. Aluminum, though stronger than wood, is relatively soft and flexible. As a result, the frames of rackets like the Prince Classic had a tendency to distort on impact, meaning that players would struggle to direct the ball precisely where they wanted, especially if they didn't hit it in the exact center of the strings. For good players, this was a huge problem—and one that wasn't nearly compensated for by the other benefits. The upshot was that pros didn't immediately join amateurs in making the switch to larger rackets.[9] (A sixteen-year-old Pam Shriver used the Prince Classic to reach the 1978 US Open final, but she was an exception.) Wooden rackets still provided the best feel and control, which is why most of the era's most skillful players— McEnroe, Borg, Navratilova, Evert—continued using them throughout the seventies and into the early eighties.

Soon, however, another breakthrough occurred, this time definitive: rackets began to be constructed from composites. Fiber-reinforced polymers, as man-made composites are technically known, consist of woven strips of synthetic fiber bonded with a plastic resin. The first synthetic composite— fiberglass—was developed in the 1930s; in the late sixties it was joined by carbon fiber (sometimes called "graphite fiber") and Kevlar. Composites are stronger and stiffer than metals like aluminum and steel; they don't corrode so easily; they can be molded into a greater variety of shapes; in many cases they can withstand intense heat; and, crucially, they are lightweight. Such qualities make them ideal for equipment that needs to be strong, durable, and portable.

Today, composites are the main element in a wide variety of high-performance products, including airplane wings and fuselages, military vehicles such as Humvees, spacecraft heat shields and launch vehicles, boat hulls, and swimming pool

---

9. This may well be the reason the authorities were so laissez-faire about the switch to larger heads: it was thought at the time that they wouldn't make much difference to the game, because they wouldn't prove attractive to pros.

panels. And they have also revolutionized—or at least significantly affected—a host of sports. Most items of equipment that were once made from wood or metal are now made wholly or partly from composite. Fiberglass was introduced as a coating for surfboards in the late 1940s. The first fiberglass-coated skis appeared in the early 1960s. Graphite shafts for golf clubs started appearing in the early 1970s, though the pros only adopted them in the 1990s. Fiberglass fishing rods were common from the 1950s and were replaced, in turn, by carbon ones in the late 1970s. Formula 1 racing cars have been constructed from carbon fiber since the early 1980s, dramatically improving performance and safety. Modern table tennis bats contain a strip of carbon sandwiched between the layers of wood. The list goes on. In fact, there aren't many equipment-dependent sports that haven't seen wood or metal replaced with composite. The three most notable exceptions are cricket (where nonwillow bats were outlawed in 1978), baseball (where, mainly for safety reasons, non-wooden bats have never been permitted in the major leagues, though they are widely used in lower echelons of the sport), and snooker.

The first composite to be used in tennis rackets was fiberglass: the Head Competition, with which Arthur Ashe won Wimbledon in 1975, was made, for example, from a mix of fiberglass and aluminum. However, the truly significant development—the switch to "graphite," as rackets made from a carbon fiber-based composite mix tended to be known—took place around the start of the eighties. Graphite neatly overcame the limitations of previous materials. Its stiffness, much greater than that of fiberglass alone, meant that there weren't problems with distortion. Unlike wood, it was strong enough to support bigger heads. And—of great significance in the long term—graphite rackets were lighter than their wooden and aluminum predecessors. The early ones weren't actually that light by today's standards. The Dunlop Maxplay 200G, released in 1982 and used by McEnroe and Graf, weighed what now seems an incredibly hefty 12.5 ounces. But that was still considerably less than the 13.5 ounces or even 14 ounces that was common for wooden rackets. And besides, as composite technology improved, graphite frames became progressively lighter. Today, an unstrung racket weighing 11 ounces is regarded as on the heavy side, and some weigh as little as 9 ounces.[10]

Once graphite arrived, there was no turning back. Within two or three years, wooden rackets had virtually disappeared and aluminum was now only used to make cheap rackets for inexperienced players. (Today titanium, an even lighter metal, is often used for entry-level rackets.) A few pro players, including Gabriela Sabatini, persisted with "woodies"—frames that combined wood and graphite—until the mideighties, but they, too, then switched to all-composite frames. The "graphite revolution" was complete.

---

10. The unstrung weight of Federer's racket—12 ounces—is heavier than that of any other top player. Before his switch to a larger head in 2014, he also used a racket with a smaller head—90 square inches—than that of any other top pro. His racket, in other words, though composite, was the closest on tour to an old-school wooden one in terms of weight and head size.

5.

How, exactly, did the new rackets change tennis? It's well known that the sport became faster and more powerful once graphite took over. From this, it's often assumed that the new rackets themselves must have been much more powerful than the old ones, enabling players to strike the ball harder. But this isn't quite right. On account of their greater stiffness and larger heads, graphite rackets may indeed have been slightly more powerful, overall, than the rackets they supplanted, though on the other hand they were lighter, and lightness decreases a racket's power.[11] But this isn't *why* the sport speeded up.

It's important to remember that, in tennis, generating power is not difficult for good players. They can hit the ball hard more or less whichever racket they use. The challenge has always been to generate power *while keeping the ball in*. Tennis is different from sports like cricket or baseball, where power is what might be termed an unequivocal good. For a batsman in cricket or a baseball hitter, there is almost never

---

11. It is an oddity of tennis research that the question of the relative power of wooden and graphite rackets has never been satisfactorily cleared up. As things stand, the closest thing to a scientific study was the comparative test carried out by *Tennis* magazine in 1997, when Mark Philippoussis was measured hitting first serves both with his normal racket and a classic wooden one. With his normal racket, he averaged 124 mph, and with the wooden one, 122 mph. In other words, there was very little difference. Interestingly, though, Philippoussis got a significantly higher percentage of deliveries in when serving with his normal racket, although this may just have been because he was used to playing with it.

a downside to hitting the ball hard. Generally, the faster and further the ball goes, the more runs will be scored, the more home runs made. This is why a powerful cricket bat will always be preferable to a less powerful one, assuming other attributes, such as weight and balance, are equal.

But in tennis, power *is* equivocal. A hard shot may be more effective than a less powerful one, but only if it lands in. And hitting the ball hard makes that less likely to happen. Power and consistency, in other words, tend to work against one another. For this reason, it is possible for a tennis racket to be too powerful. If designers came up with some snazzy innovation that instantly doubled a racket's power, no one would buy it, because the loss of control would be too great. By contrast, a twice-as-powerful cricket bat, assuming it were legal, would be guaranteed to be an instant hit.

It follows that an increase in power in tennis is not necessarily caused by an increase in racket power. Just as likely—in fact, more likely—is players striking their shots harder because the racket allows them to exert better control. This is the key to understanding the impact of graphite rackets: rather than being more powerful themselves, what they did was to hugely expand the possibilities for control. In tennis, there are three basic methods for ensuring the ball goes in. One is to hit the ball accurately—which, in practice, means keeping it within the sidelines (relatively easy) and (the greater challenge) at the right height over the net (i.e., low enough not to go long but high enough to clear it). The second method is to hit the ball gently. The less power in a shot, the more quickly gravity will act upon the ball and bring it down inside the court. (Doing this also has the advantage of making it easier to be accurate.) The third, more technically challenging, option is to interfere with the ball's natural flight path through the motion of your racket. In other words, to use spin.

There are two main types of spin in tennis: slice and topspin. Slice, or backspin, is achieved by hitting the ball with a downward, "slicing" motion while tilting the racket face slightly upwards. The effect of slice is to make the ball hang in the air for longer—giving it the appearance of floating over the net. When a sliced ball hits the ground, it keeps low and skids off the court. It also rebounds off the opponent's racket in a downward direction, making it likely to hit the net unless the player adjusts his or her swing. Strictly speaking, slice on its own does not increase control: because the ball stays in the air for longer, misdirected slice shots can easily drift long. But equally, because they tend to be relatively gentle, and good players are able to direct them low over the net, they are usually fairly safe. Topspin is achieved, conversely, by hitting with an upward motion and "brushing up" the back of the ball with the racket head tilted slightly forward. Whereas slice makes the ball hang, topspin makes it dip down sharply. Instead of skidding upon bouncing, it rears up and then rebounds off the opponent's racket in an upward direction. Hitting with topspin *does* significantly increase control, because the ball's up-and-down trajectory means that it can easily clear the net and still land safely in the court. Topspin, in other words, makes being accurate less important.

The reason graphite rackets had such an effect on tennis is that they made hitting with topspin—and not just any topspin, but *heavy* topspin—considerably easier than it had been. Although topspin was a feature of the game in the pregraphite era, by today's standards it was seldom heavy and it was also just one of a number of baseline options. Lots of players—in fact most—hit the majority of their ground strokes flat, or with slice, even on the forehand side. Because of this, players had to rely much more on the first two methods for achieving control: being accurate, and not hitting the ball too hard. The gentleness of tennis in the precomposite era is often a source of puzzlement today: to eyes grown accustomed to the power and pace of the modern game, it seems extraordinary that the world's top players could ever have been so cautious. But once it's understood that heavy topspin wasn't available then as it is now, the slowness of pregraphite-era tennis becomes much more comprehensible. It's not that Rosewall, Drobny, Laver, et al. were fundamentally incapable of blasting the ball, it's just that, lacking the ability to impart huge amounts of topspin, they needed to play more carefully to ensure their shots went in.

The crucial factor in the topspin-generating capabilities of the new rackets wasn't overall head size but head width. The faces of wooden rackets typically measured nine inches across. This meant that brushing up the back of the ball—the method for producing topspin—required great precision. If the player's judgment wasn't spot-on, the ball wouldn't meet the center of the racket (and wooden rackets, remember, had tiny sweet spots) or, even more damagingly, it would clip the frame. The new rackets were initially an inch or so wider—a small-sounding difference, but sufficient to make hitting with a sharp upward brushing motion considerably easier. The larger sweet spot was easier to locate, and there was much less chance of the ball clipping the frame. Suddenly, from requiring immense precision, hitting consistently with significant topspin became something most players could achieve.

Head size wasn't the whole story. The new rackets were also lighter—and, as the technology developed, they became progressively more so. With a lighter racket, it is natural to swing faster, and a fast swing not only increases power, but also intensifies spin. As players swung faster, they found that their shots were becoming both more powerful and—thanks to the increased spin that resulted—more consistent. Thus swinging really fast and sharply upwards became not the risky strategy it had been but the most effective means of ensuring the ball consistently landed in. For the first time in the game's history, a virtuous circle was established, whereby power and control were not adversaries but allies. Topspin became not an optional extra—one possible strategy among many—but the bedrock of the professional game.[12]

6.

Once players discovered that they had more spin and power at their disposal, backcourt play became significantly more

12. For a good summary of the physics behind these developments, see "The Inch That Changed Tennis Forever" by Rod Cross, *Tennis Industry* magazine, January 2006.

aggressive. In the old days, baseline rallies had largely been about attrition. When players forced the pace, their main objective wasn't to win the point outright but to set up an opportunity to come to the net. Even short balls were rarely hit for winners. Overall, there was a clear distinction between attack and defense. Attack-minded players (such as McEnroe and Navratilova) looked to come to the net as much as possible, as that was the only way—short of hitting an ace or unreturnable serve—to finish points off quickly. Defensive players (Borg, Evert) stayed on the baseline and aimed to peg back/frustrate their opponents, eventually drawing an error or, failing that, passing or lobbing them when they came to the net.

At a certain point, however, this distinction between forecourt-based attack and backcourt-based defense began to blur. Arguably, it was Connors who first showed that it was possible to be highly aggressive while playing mainly from the baseline. As a young player in the seventies, and armed with his T2000, he regularly thrashed older, craftier opponents—notably Ken Rosewall in the 1974 Wimbledon final—by pretty much blasting them off the court. However, Connors's style can't be described as truly modern, because his shots were almost completely flat: he relied on low net clearance, rather than topspin, to achieve consistency. It wasn't until a decade or so after this that the hard-hitting, modern backcourt style that would come to be known as the "power baseline game" emerged—thanks, above all, to Ivan Lendl.

Lendl, as Wallace pointed out, was the "first top pro whose strokes and tactics appeared to be designed round the special capacities of the composite racket." His approach was based on bossing points with a forehand that combined ferocious power with heavy topspin. He could hit clean winners from the baseline and—rather like Federer—he regularly backed away to his left, creating space to hit both inside-out and inside-in forehands. He was also the first player, with the exception of Borg (whose game, too, in some ways preempted the power baseline era), to fetishize his own athleticism. Lendl trained harder than anyone else—and his resulting physical toughness was crucial to his success. This isn't coincidental. The power baseline game, to a much greater extent than its predecessors, was a style founded on strength and endurance. Players had to be able to cope with long baseline rallies played at breakneck speed. Even the shot mechanics were considerably more grueling, with players regularly taking balls up around their chests and rotating their upper bodies (and, eventually, leaving the ground as they swung). It was a style purpose-built for the sport's new era of ultraprofessionalism.

It was around the start of the nineties that the power baseline style really took off, with the emergence of the Chang/Courier/Muster/Agassi generation. (Throughout the second half of the previous decade, Lendl had plowed a somewhat lonely, though hugely successful, furrow.) These players all hit their ground strokes powerfully and with heavy topspin and, like Lendl, were exceptionally fit. It can't be a coincidence that they were also the sport's first true postwood generation, having spent their formative years playing exclusively with composite rackets. The other distinctive thing about them was that their shots were strikingly similar. This point is crucial to understanding the effect the power baseline game has had on the sport's character. For it didn't just limit players' options *strategically*, in the sense of making net play much less common; it also reduced the game's variety *technically*, because it necessitated the widespread adoption of a new, and somewhat limited, set of techniques.

These techniques were dictated not only by the need to produce topspin, but also the need to defend against it. As we've seen, heavy topspin, among other things, makes the ball rear up off the court. Therefore, the new techniques had to be geared not just to brushing up the back of the ball but to coping with balls that bounced high. On the forehand wing, these two imperatives neatly came together in the development of the "modern" forehand—the shot that virtually all of today's professionals use. Various features distinguish the modern forehand from its "classic" forerunner, notably its much more "extreme" (or "western" or "frying pan") grip, its open stance, and the use of significant torso rotation.

The path taken by the backhand was inevitably different. Unlike the forehand, the single-hander wasn't a shot that could be revamped for the modern age, because it can only be played one way: side on, with the weight on the front leg and with a reasonably upright grip. (It is, you could say, inherently classic.)[13] What happened instead, of course, was that a totally different stroke—the two-hander—massively grew in

---

13. This isn't to say that the single-hander offers no scope for grip variation. Some players—for instance, Justine Henin—have successfully played the shot with an "extreme," or semiwestern, grip.

popularity and ended up all but supplanting the one-hander. For most players, the two-handed backhand (which, for right handers, is mechanically somewhat similar to a left-handed forehand) is better suited to the demands of modern tennis: it is a more consistent and stable shot than the single-hander, therefore more useful in bruising baseline rallies, and is much better for coping with high-bouncing balls.

These technical changes, however, came with a cost: aesthetically, the game deteriorated. Not only is the double-handed backhand a much less graceful and natural-looking shot than the single-hander, but the modern forehand is inherently less elegant than the classic stroke. The latter—hit side on and with an upright grip and a smooth upward swing—was a lovely, measured shot. By contrast, the modern forehand—so explosive and dynamic—tends to resemble a pummel or a slap. Grip is key to this: once the hand gets shifted round the handle to the point where it is almost underneath it, the elbow naturally comes forward at the point of impact, and the shot almost always must be hit with a crooked arm and with the body awkwardly twisted round. This—as Djokovic's forehand plainly demonstrates—is not particularly conducive to elegance.

7.

In the nineties, despite its growing success, the power baseline game didn't have the run of the park. Serve and volley remained a major force in men's tennis—less so in women's—

especially on fast surfaces. The dominant player of the decade, after all, was Pete Sampras; and Goran Ivanisevic and Richard Krajicek both won Wimbledon. In fact, somewhat ironically, the nineties are now considered to be something of a golden age for serve and volley, and players who rush the net nowadays are often described as playing in a "nineties style."

The truth, however, is more nuanced. Nineties'-style serve and volleying, as practiced by Sampras, Rafter, et al., was actually significantly different to the serve and volleying of previous eras, in that it was much more dependent on the serve. The game's balance of power, after all, had already shifted towards the baseline. But something else had also been happening: serving had improved.[14] Increasingly, to get into the net, players needed the insurance policy of a highly dominant serve. The objectives of serve and volley had become at least partially defensive: it was a way to take an opponent's ground strokes out of the equation. The aim was to win the point with a quick knockout blow (ideally a straightforward putaway set up by the initial delivery). The days when players could drift into the net behind a middling serve or a speculative approach shot and still expect to win the point in three or four volleys—as the likes of Laver or McEnroe often did—were gone. It was either a clean, quick kill, or nothing.

---

14. As we've seen, graphite rackets provided better control, and this applied to serves as well as groundstrokes. Players, as a result, were able to strike their serves harder while still reliably getting them in. But this isn't the only reason serving got better. Improved overall athleticism played a part and also, crucially, height: the average height of top male tennis players has increased by about four inches since the sixties. Height matters to serving because a higher hitting point gives a better trajectory for getting the ball in the service box (and so again makes it possible to strike the shot harder) and because the steeper bounce makes for an awkward return. The huge advantage really tall players have on serve can be seen from the fact that the three top slots in the all-time list for percentage of service games won are occupied by Ivo Karkovic (6' 11"), Milos Raonic (6' 5") and John Isner (6' 10"). On the other hand, tall players generally move less well. To judge from the last decade, the optimal current height for an elite male tennis player is between 6' 1" (Nadal's and Federer's height) and 6' 3" (Murray's).

Once nineties' serve and volley is understood in these terms—as a partially defensive tactic predicated on big serving—its subsequent disappearance becomes less mysterious. The more dependent serve and volley becomes on the serve, the more its value as a strategy becomes questionable. If a serve and volleyer *has* to rely on his serve to win him the majority of his points, he may start to feel that there isn't necessarily all that much point in coming to the net. The overall context is important here. As ground strokes became more powerful and effective, they were able to do more of the point-finishing work previously done by volleys. Players whose serves regularly elicited short returns could be confident of ending the point with one or two heavy backcourt blows. At the same time, returns of serve—like all ground strokes—were becoming better, making the first volley, very often, a tougher shot. In such circumstances, coming to the net, far from producing a tangible advantage, looked increasingly like a way of exposing yourself to unnecessary risk.[15]

Men's tennis in the nineties can be seen as a contest between big-serving serve and volleyers and orthodox power baseliners—and it was the latter group that ultimately pre-

---

15. This wasn't the only reason for the dramatic falling away of serve and volley in the early 2000s. Two other factors played a part: the slowing down of court surfaces, including at Wimbledon, largely in order to counter the over-dominant serve; and the rise of co-poly strings, which enabled players to get more bite and dip on returns and passing shots, making coming to the net still more challenging. However, important as both these factors were, I think serve and volley would have substantially declined anyway, thanks to the developments discussed in this chapter. Graphite rackets had already shifted the orientation of the sport towards the baseline. Big serving prolonged the life of serve and volley, but it is doubtful whether it would have done so indefinitely.

vailed. In effect, the big servers laid down their rackets and said: "Hang on a minute, why don't we just become power baseliners, *too*?" This is, perhaps, the real measure of the triumph of the power baseline style: it shattered the link that had long existed between strong serving and net play. And so the last, unloved exponents of "boom-boom" tennis—the Samprases, Ivanesevices, and Krajiceks of the nineties—transmogrified into the big-serving baseliners—the Isners, Raonics, and Janowiczes—of the new millennium. More or less everyone now played from the back.

8.

Arriving at any kind of overall verdict on modern tennis is, as I've suggested, extremely tricky. At virtually every stage, the arguments cut both ways. The decline of net play has undoubtedly been a loss. Unless things change in some unexpected way—which, of course, is perfectly possible—we will never again witness, at the highest level, a match like the 1980 men's Wimbledon final, when McEnroe, an out-and-out serve and volleyer, took on Borg, an out-and-out baseliner. And few people would claim that this is a good thing.

On the other hand, it's easy to idealize the past. Not long ago, I watched a recording of the 1969 Wimbledon final between Rod Laver and John Newcombe. Both players came to the net behind every single serve (in stark contrast to the 2002 final between Lleyton Hewitt and David Nalbandian, when, famously, neither player served-and-volleyed once).

And what was striking was how boring it was. The rallies were short and predictable. The server would come in, and would either win the point in two or three shots, or would get lobbed or passed. The whole match had an unvarying staccato rhythm. I'm not sure it was preferable to Hewitt–Nalbandian, let alone Federer–Nadal. (That said, I was watching it with the benefit of hindsight: I could compare it with later iterations of the sport. The spectators who watched it at the time had no knowledge of Federer–Nadal, just as we have no idea what the Wimbledon final of 2050 will be like).

The baseline contests of old could also be pretty deadly. What Wallace described as the "moon ball tedium of baseline attrition" was often associated with the women's game, but it wasn't entirely absent on the men's side, especially on slow courts, where rallies would sometimes go on for minutes.[16] Something that critics of modern tennis forget is that, in a sense, the classic game needed net play, because baseline rallies on their own were too ponderous to sustain interest. This isn't so much the case anymore. The fast-paced, explosive baseline rallies of today are often enthralling—which makes the reduction in net play less of a cross to bear.

Topspin, too, is double-edged. Although rallies consisting entirely of topspin shots can be repetitive, the use of spin also opens up new strategic possibilities. Armed with topspin, players can create sharper angles from the backcourt, another reason why volleying becomes less necessary. The booming forehand winner is just one aspect of the modern game; there

16. Punch "Borg Vilas long rally" into YouTube to see an example.

are also the deft angled shots, the subtle calibrations of pace and spin. Although players move back and forward less than they used to, they cover more ground sideways (and do so faster), and also use net clearance in more inventive ways. Some of the sport's strategic variety, in other words, has migrated away from the forecourt to the lateral and vertical planes.

Yet there is one accusation that can be leveled at the modern game that is—or at least was—virtually unanswerable. This is that the shots themselves have become less attractive. Following the switch to graphite rackets, as we've seen, ground-stroke technique changed in various ways—and the aesthetic fallout was considerable. The requirement to impart immense power and topspin meant that shots were no longer as natural, as smooth, as they had been. They became more brutal and jarring. Tennis, in consequence, got uglier. By the early nineties, this was already a major problem for the sport, and it certainly played a big part in my own disillusionment with it. By the early years of the new millennium, the problem seemed more intractable still: the decline of serve and volleying meant that there was now even less strategic variation than there had been in the previous decade. Men's tennis, in fact, seemed trapped in a cul-de-sac. This sentiment, widespread at the time, was captured by a letter that appeared in the *New York Times* in September 2002:

> Mike Freeman's proposal that what men's tennis needs most is a "strong marketing force" would be akin to promoting the emperor's new clothes: there's just noth-

ing there! No amount of marketing can erase the real problem with men's tennis, which is that it has become a dull, homogenized power game resulting from high-tech, oversized rackets.

The only effective solution, as proposed by John McEnroe, would be a return to wooden rackets, which would bring back touch, strategy, finesse, and a variety of competitive styles to men's pro tennis.

It says something about the glorious unpredictability of sport—and about Federer's impact—that the view expressed in this letter seems unthinkable now. Within a year of it being written, of course, the Swiss had begun his reign of dominance.

9.

Roger Federer made tennis beautiful again. And he did this while playing a version of the power baseline game. It's as if he bottled the gracefulness that belonged to the sport's earlier eras and decanted it into the modern style. There is, for this reason, a quality of the unreal about him. He defied the logic of four decades' worth of change. Everything pointed to a future in which he (or someone like him) would be impossible. And yet not only did he exist, he managed to excel.

That Federer is an exception is apparent in all sorts of ways. It's there, for example, in the variety and subtlety of his play; in the fact that he moves around the court with such ease. But it's also evident—and this is the really crucial point—in the way his shots *look*. Federer found a way to make heavy topspin ground strokes look smooth and graceful—an achievement that, to me, seems almost unfathomable. As has often been said, part of the reason his shots are so attractive is that they appear to be somewhat old-fashioned. And yet there is nothing remotely old school about what he does with the ball. There's a kind of paradox here. How can it be resolved?

I'll ignore the backhand, because that wing, while it contributes significantly to the visual appeal of Federer's game, doesn't pose any significant explanatory problems. Federer's backhand appears somewhat old-fashioned because the single-hander is a technically retrograde shot; and when played well, it invariably looks good. More important—and interesting—is the forehand. This shot is the key to Federer's game strategically—with the possible exception of the serve, it's what wins him most of his points—and goes a long way to explaining why his tennis looks as it does.

Federer's forehand is in many respects a mechanically orthodox modern stroke. Compare it to the forehands of Djokovic or Nadal, and the same basic elements are there. Yet there is no denying that, in some subtle, hard-to-define way, it looks different. It is of the modern game and yet not of it. At this point, we need to get a bit specific. The unusualness of Federer's forehand starts with his grip. He uses what some analysts describe as a "modified eastern" grip—or, one could say, an eastern grip with semiwestern attributes. I won't go into the technicalities, but the basic point is that, in an incredibly precise way, Federer locates his hand position on the border between traditionalism and modernity, conservatism and extremity (or at least to the extent that those qualities can be reflected in the bevels of a racket handle). There's a sense in which his grip can go either way, be old or new, one thing or the other.

This is highly important. Grip makes a big difference to what players can do with the ball, and to what their shots look like. A modest rotation of the hand round the handle—just a fraction of an inch either way—will dramatically alter the whole aspect of a stroke. The conventional wisdom holds that, depending on where players place their grips on the handle, they will gain some advantages and some disadvantages. For instance, a more extreme, or rotated, grip makes it easier to brush up the ball and hit it at chest height but hinders taking it low or early. Yet Federer has managed to evade such limitations, and a lot of this has to do with his shape-shifting grip. Because of its hybrid, one-thing-nor-the-other nature, he can, in effect, go conservative or extreme with the shot; he can combine the best of both worlds. This results in an unprecedented flexibility. He can hit balls up high just as easily as down low, he is happy to take them early or late, and he can likewise produce massive variations of spin.[17]

---

17. Given this, one might ask: Why don't all players use the same grip as Federer? The answer is that it's not so simple. To use Federer's grip successfully requires incredible timing and skill. And virtually all juniors today are taught a more extreme grip. On the other hand, maybe things are changing. Grigor Dimitrov—or, as he was known, "Baby Fed"—uses the same grip as Federer. Just recently, too, one of the best sixteen-year-olds in Britain (who also happens to be the son of the head coach at my club) told me that he had adjusted his forehand grip in order to make it more conservative, more like Federer's: he believed this would give him more options.

The unusualness of Federer's grip feeds into his forehand in other ways. One element of this is arm position. In 2006, the tennis writer and coach John Yandell subjected Federer's forehand to intensive high-speed video analysis, and noticed that his arm positions vary far more than those of other players.[18] Whether your arm is straight or not when you hit a forehand depends largely on your grip. The further the hand rotates round the handle, the more elbow bend (and also wrist bend) there has to be in the stroke. A more upright, traditional grip, by contrast, naturally results in a straight arm—which was how the shot tended to be played in wooden racket days.

Most players today hit their forehands with bent elbows pretty much all the time, and don't significantly vary the position of their wrists. But Federer, Yandell pointed out, constantly moves between different elbow and wrist positions, and also varies them in relation to his degree of torso rotation. (Yandell counted at least twenty distinct variations to Federer's forehand; most players have no more than three or four.) Much of the time he plays his forehand with a straight arm—but not always. And because the angle of his wrist varies significantly, too, as well as his body position, the shot's flexibility is massively extended in terms of how high or low he can comfortably strike the ball, the degree of spin, the amount of pace, and where he can direct it. Federer is uniquely able, off his forehand wing, to hit the ball to pretty

18. Yandell's full account of his research, "Roger Federer and the Evolution of the Modern Forehand," can be read on his website, www.tennisplayer.net.

much any part of the court, with every conceivable variation of height, spin, and power; and he can do this from any position. For Yandell, the stroke is the "best of all worlds," offering the "advantages of both the classical and extreme styles without the limitations of either."

Something else that's distinctive about Federer's technique is his head position. As has often been observed, he turns it towards the ball much more than other players, and is more or less alone in actually watching the ball at the moment of impact. (Most players focus on a spot just in front of the racket.) Even after Federer has made contact, his head stays turned round for a moment longer, as if he were freezing the shot in his mind. Yandell is unsure whether or not this confers any benefits. (He suggests it may actually explain why Federer gets more "shanks," or mishits, than other players.) But whatever it does for the effectiveness of Federer's tennis, it certainly contributes to its elegance. As ground strokes became more dynamic and explosive in the eighties and nineties, a certain sense of poise, of stillness, that was inherent in the old techniques, was lost. Federer's forehand has plenty of dynamism, but, in the way he turns his head right round and carefully, almost tenderly, looks at the ball, there is, too, a lingering trace of an earlier age's side-on stillness.

10.

These technical features, when considered together, go some way to explaining the distinct visual impression that Federer's forehand creates. I would describe this impression as a kind of elegant discordance, a feeling of parts moving smoothly in opposite directions. One aspect of Federer's forehand that's very noticeable is that he often seems to fall away from the ball. This is counterintuitive: conventional wisdom insists that the one place a tennis player's weight shouldn't go when striking a ball is backwards. Yet this impression of falling away is a kind of illusion, a product of the capacity Federer's body seems to have of moving in two different directions at once. On the one hand, his torso rotates round to the left, opening right up in the process (as is standard); on the other hand, his (normally straight) arm, wrist and head all stay behind, and somehow move out towards the ball. With Federer, the forehand isn't so much a rotation, or an uncoiling, as an opening out, and this is why the movement appears to be flowing rather than muscular. Energy is dissipated rather than forced in one direction; the shot has a molten, liquid quality.[19] Federer's forehand is the most beautiful shot in the history of tennis. And it may also be the most effective.

---

19. A "great liquid whip" was Wallace's description.

2011–2013

My girlfriend and I got married in 2011. A few months later, in October, our first child—a son—was born. It might be assumed that the switch to a more settled existence would have taken the edge off my ardor for Federer, relegated him to a firm second (or, indeed, third) place. But my feelings remained as powerful as ever. Instead of fading, they just took a slightly different form, accommodated themselves to the new presences in my life.

Federer turned thirty in 2011. It proved, on the whole, a frustrating year. For the most part, he played well, but he wasn't terribly successful. For the first time since 2002, he failed to win a Grand Slam and his ranking slid to No. 3. There was bad luck involved: he lost some exceptionally close matches, none more so than the spectacularly ghastly Djokovic semifinal at Flushing Meadow, when, for the second year in succession, he lost after holding two match points. (And this time, moreover, they were on his serve.) He also kept coming up against opponents in the form of their lives—as was the case with Jo-Wilfried Tsonga at Wimbledon. Nor were matters helped by the fact that he now had to contend not just with Nadal but with a newly formidable Djokovic, who went unbeaten for the first five months of the year, a run of forty-three matches that only came to an end when Federer beat him, magically, in the semifinal at Roland Garros.

With a second player threatening to eclipse him (and Murray also making a strong bid), Federer, at this point, was again being written off. But he responded—thrillingly—by powering back to No. 1. It all started at the end of 2011, when he suddenly won three tournaments in a row: Basel, Paris, and the World Tour Finals. I saw him thrash Nadal 6–3, 6–0 at the last of these events—this was just three weeks after my son was born. Nadal wasn't at his best, but it was nonetheless immensely pleasing to see Federer rampant against his old rival. His revival continued in the early months of 2012, with triumphs at Rotterdam, Dubai, and Indian Wells (where he again beat Nadal). He went on to win on the ill-fated blue clay in Madrid before, in July, lifting his seventh Wimbledon crown, dispatching Murray in the final. A wave of patriotism was sweeping the nation—it was the summer of the London Olympics—and a Brit hadn't won the men's trophy since Fred Perry in 1936. Was this, finally, "our" year? I remained immune to such sentiments. I admire Murray, and, in other circumstances, I would have been happy for him to win, but whatever patriotic feelings I had—and I don't, nowadays, have all that many—were never going to make a dent in my loyalty to Federer.

Federer's Wimbledon win got him back to world No. 1. A couple of months later, he broke Sampras's record for the number of total weeks in the top spot. He retained the ranking until November, at which point he was again surpassed by Djokovic. Things at this point still looked positive—he ended the season playing well enough. There was no indication of what was to come.

The following year, it goes without saying, was easily the bleakest year of my Federer-obsessed life. Something peculiar, unaccountable, happened. After a promising enough start (the semis in Australia), Federer's form dipped precipitously, reaching a nadir in the middle stretch of the season, when he lost in the second round of Wimbledon to Sergiy Stakhovsky—a player ranked more than a hundred places below him—and then in the last sixteen at the US Open to Tommy Robredo, a journeyman he'd brushed aside in all eleven of their previous meetings. That defeat was the worst of all. Robredo wasn't even playing particularly well, he was just doing what he always did. It was as if Federer had misplaced his game; the shots looked more or less the same, but the brilliance, the genius, had been scooped right out. His ranking slipped from two to seven and he was doubtful for a while for the World Tour Finals.

Federer himself seemed at a loss to know what to do. After Wimbledon, he briefly experimented (unsuccessfully) with a larger-headed racket, before returning to his trusty

90-square-inch frame. He claimed many times that his form was on the verge of returning—only to suffer another humiliating loss. As the defeats piled up, pundits rushed to proclaim that the once-great Federer, at the age of thirty-two, was fading fast. Fellow players, including Djokovic, suggested that he had lost a yard of pace. Some observers argued that, by stubbornly prolonging his career, he was making himself look foolish, tarnishing his legacy. He maintained that he wasn't unduly worried, that things would get back on track, and he referred repeatedly—though somewhat elliptically—to the back injury he'd been plagued by all year. There were some suggestions that he was making this up.[20]

At the end of the year, in November, I saw Federer lose to Djokovic, in three sets, in his first group match at the World Tour Finals. I'd managed to land a press pass and, afterwards, I attended Federer's press conference. I was surprised by how tired and dispirited he looked: after all, had he really expected to beat Djokovic? He was tetchy, irascible with several of his questioners. Although his form had shown signs of picking up in recent weeks, he still wasn't anything like the Federer of old, the one I'd delighted in all these years. That night, as I left the arena, I wondered whether I would ever see that Federer again.

---

20. One tennis journalist told me that this became something of a press box joke: whenever Federer lost, he would refer to his stiff back.

chapter three

The curse of Nadal

1.

A blot appeared on the otherwise sunny vista that stretched before Federer in 2004–2006, and it took the form of a preternaturally muscled Spaniard. Like most diehard Federer fans, I loathe Rafael Nadal. I cannot stand the man or his tennis. In my more reflective moments, I am capable of admitting that this attitude falls short of perfect objectivity. Nadal, I am prepared to concede, may not be a wholly despicable human being. But no amount of ordinary decency can make up for the grave offense that he has committed, and continues to commit, simply by existing. This alone is enough to make him loathsome, unforgivable.

Yet those inclined to castigate Nadal for more run-of-the-mill failings do not lack material to work with. The list of the Spaniard's negative attributes is as extensive as it is obvious. (Still, going through it provides its own grim satisfaction: in our most abject moments, we Federer fans need something to hang on to.) Standing at the apex of the edifice of his odiousness is the attention he pays to his gluteus maximus, which he once described—as if this explained things—as being "bigger than normal." His dislodgement, prior to each point, of a (presumably?) phantom wedgie is as weird as it is unsavory, and has the unfortunate effect of conjuring up an image that I—and no doubt others—would prefer not to have to contemplate: that of the Spaniard's chronically irascible posterior.

If the shorts-tugging thing were Nadal's only quirk, that would be off-putting enough. But it's just one element in a smorgasbord of tics. In the entire history of sport, has there ever been an athlete more flagrantly OCD than Nadal, one more neurotically in thrall to his rituals and compulsions? Every second he spends on court, other than when the ball is in play, is minutely preprogrammed, robotized. Before each coin toss, he undertakes the exact same sequence of actions involving the meticulous laying down of his personal effects (tournament ID placed faceup next to his bag, which is positioned on a towel), the removal of his jacket (always facing the crowd, always accompanied by jumping), and the ingestion of a packet of energy gel (always in four squeezes). While walking around the court, he scrupulously avoids the lines, stepping over them right foot first. At changeovers, he unfailingly waits for his opponent before rounding the net post, and is never the first to leave his chair. He positions his two water bottles (one warm, one chilled) in exactly the same place, labels pointing towards the end he's about to play from. As a point approaches, the obsessiveness ratchets up a notch: the tennis writer Greg Garber identified twelve distinct phases to Nadal's preserve preparation, including toweling down in a particular way, wiping the baseline with his shoes, and then, as he bounces the ball with his racket, sequentially touching his shirt, nose, and hair. The entire ritual, according to Garber, lasts (depending on the importance of the point) 27–31 seconds, which explains why Nadal—to his unending outrage—so frequently falls afoul of the twenty-five-second time violation rule.

All this, moreover, is just the visible peak of the iceberg— the stuff that the public gets to see. There's also what happens behind closed doors. In his memoir, Nadal alludes to the "inflexible routines" he settles into before each match, which include an unvarying meal of sauceless pasta and plain fish and personally putting the grips on each of his six Babolat Aero-Pro Drive rackets. Forty-five minutes before play, he takes a freezing cold shower: "It's the first step in the last phase of what I call my pre-game ritual." (Which raises the question: just how many "phases" does this particular ritual have?) Lleyton Hewitt, commentating on one of Nadal's matches at the 2014 Australian Open, described the Spaniard repeatedly taking his shirt off and on before leaving the locker room. (Hewitt was heavily criticized for divulging this backroom tidbit.) Nadal's compulsions seem potentially limitless; where does such behavior end? Is the prematch ritual itself preceded by a pre-prematch ritual? At what point, following a victory, do preparations for the next match begin? Is any portion of Nadal's life not under the sway of some compulsion? Is the man capable of relaxing?

In his memoir, Nadal writes that the goal of his rituals is to "silence the voices in my head." The aim is to "bottle up" all "human feelings," thereby turning himself into a "tennis machine." In this sense, there's a continuity between his mental approach to tennis and the way he plays the sport, because, on court, Nadal is certainly machinelike. His game is founded not on surprise or variation but on the principle of eternal repetition. Throughout his career, Nadal's strategy has been to find what works and then keep doing it over and over, never deviating from the script. His tennis, like his whole life, is based on denial and self-negation—on resisting the temptation to do what comes naturally. Writing about the buildup to the 2008 Wimbledon final, he describes visualizing his game plan:

> I have to be centered, no distractions, do what I have to do in each moment. If I have to hit the ball twenty times to Federer's backhand, I'll hit it twenty times, not nineteen. If I go up to the net, I hit it to his backhand, not to his drive . . . Losing your concentration means going to the net and hitting the ball to his forehand, or omitting in a rush of blood to serve to his backhand—always to his backhand—or going for a winner when it's not time. Being concentrated means keeping doing what you know you have to do, never changing your plan, unless the

circumstances of a rally or of the game change exceptionally . . . It means discipline, it means holding back when
the temptation arises to go for broke.

This is about as close to Stoicism as a sporting philosophy can
get. Having deployed his tics and rituals to quash his "human
feelings," Nadal is able to play the tennis of an automaton,
relentlessly, joylessly sticking to his "plan."

Quite aside from his personality and playing style, a third
avenue of Nadal opprobrium is open to Federer fans in the
unedifying facts of the Spaniard's biography. No successful
tennis career ever seems preordained—the odds are always
stacked against the boy growing up to become a champion—
but in Nadal's case, the path to greatness proved especially
rocky and obstacle-laden. His life teems with crossroads and
turning points—moments where, had the stars been aligned
differently, his dreams of greatness might have been snuffed
out. For Federer fans, such moments are painful to contemplate.

In the first place, he was born in Mallorca on June 3,
1986. Couldn't his parents have delayed the event by a
few years? He was right-handed. Ninety-nine times out of
a hundred—in fact, nine hundred and ninety-nine times
out of a thousand—right-handed children grow up to be
right-handed tennis players. But not Nadal. Uncle Toni,
Nadal's stony-faced coach—who bears a sizable portion of
the blame for every Nadal-related ill in the world—took it
upon himself, when Nadal was ten, to force his charge to
play left-handed. He did this solely because he reckoned it

would make his nephew a more awkward opponent. It is impossible not to have a certain grudging respect for the sheer courage, and the diabolical prescience, of this decision, which could, after all, have catastrophically backfired. What if, aged fifteen, Nadal had realized that he would never make it as a leftie? Having missed several critical years of right-handed development, his career would have already been finished. Aged twelve, Rafa approached another fork in the road: football or tennis? He was gifted at the former, and it was even more the family sport than tennis: another uncle, Miguel Ángel, was a Spanish international. How welcome, in retrospect, Spain would have been to Rafa's footballing talents! But, alas, he opted for tennis.

Since turning pro, too, Nadal has repeatedly flirted with oblivion. In his late teens, he suffered a mysterious recurring stress fracture in his left foot, which twice forced him to take lengthy time-offs, including the entire clay court season in 2004. After a succession of doctors had pronounced themselves baffled, a specialist in Madrid finally diagnosed the problem: Nadal had a rare congenital condition that had caused a bone in the bridge of the foot, the tarsal scaphoid, to become deformed. There was a serious risk that he'd never play competitively again. Not surprisingly, he was shattered. "I'd lie for hours on end on the sofa staring into space, or sit in the bathroom, or on the stairs, weeping. I didn't laugh, I didn't smile, I didn't want to talk. I lost all appetite for life." Nadal's only hope, the specialist said, was to tinker with the soles of his tennis shoe, in the hope of cushioning the defective area. Amazingly, this far-fetched-seeming solution worked: Nike devised a "wider and higher" shoe, and Nadal was soon back on court. Since then, while his ankle has rarely troubled him, the rest of his body has proved anything but sturdy. Twice, he has been forced out for months by tendonitis in the knees. He has suffered blisters, groin strains, shoulder strains, back spasms. A right-wrist injury led to a three-month layoff in 2014. Then no sooner had he returned than he came down with appendicitis. Every few months, it seems, a new bodily infirmity reveals itself, a fresh locus of weakness. Physically, Nadal seems permanently on the brink of collapse.

Yet the thing about him is that he never does collapse. He goes away, recuperates, and then—incredibly—comes back stronger. With Nadal, it's always the same: that odd combination of fallibility and fortitude; an endlessly repeated cycle. Down in a rally, he comes up with an impossible pass. Down in a match, he raises his game to new heights. His powers of rebound are freakish, unprecedented; the man is unbreakable, immovable, unputdownable. You almost feel that, if his body weren't as creaky as it is, he'd start inflicting injuries upon himself, merely to reproduce the conditions of adversity in which he flourishes. Perhaps this is ultimately the point of his rituals: they're not so much to silence the voices in his head as to place yet another obstacle in his path. There has never been a champion more *burdened* than Nadal, one who makes winning appear less straightforward. The crown rests heavily on his head. And although I know it doesn't reflect well on me to say it, this makes me dislike him all the more.

2.

In a sense, however, Nadal was necessary. Even I can see that. Without him, men's tennis would have become anodyne, predictable. Federer would have dominated for much longer than he did, racked up many more Grand Slams, including, probably, at least four French Opens. (How many majors altogether: twenty-four, twenty-five, twenty-six?) His success would have come to seem unlimited—which is dangerous. He would have been uncherished, resented. And tennis would have been deprived of one of its great rivalries. Yes, the sport has undoubtedly benefitted from the coexistence of Nadal and Federer, figures so different as to be virtually diametrically opposite ideals of what a tennis player should be. But I do wish things could have been more even—that the Spaniard could have won less often, and the Swiss a bit more.

Miami 2004 was when they first met. Federer was twenty-two, Nadal seventeen. Federer wasn't long into his reign of dominance: he'd won Wimbledon the previous July and then the World Master Cup in November and the Australian Open in January, displacing Andy Roddick as World No. 1. His record for the year (this was March) was 23–1. Nadal was ranked No. 34. He'd made his pro-debut aged fifteen, winning his very first match. The next year, he'd won two Challenger titles and reached the third round both at Roland Garros and at Wimbledon. He was clearly precocious, a phenomenon in the making, but he wasn't expected to trouble Federer. In his memoir, Nadal writes that he rated his chances of beating the Swiss as "scarcely above zero." Hardly anyone would have disagreed.

Yet Nadal won in less than an hour. Federer was well below his best: he'd suffered heatstroke at Indian Wells a week earlier, which had hampered his preparation. But a psychological blow must have been struck. I didn't watch the match at the time—this was before my obsession took root—but I have done since, and what's striking is how like a microcosm of their rivalry it is: all the major themes are already in place. Nadal's defensive capabilities unsettle Federer. In the fourth game, he pulls off one of his familiar Houdini acts, scampering from side to side, retrieving several impossible-looking balls before finishing the point with an on-the-run forehand. The assuredness drains from Federer's play. He no longer seems to know how to balance defense and attack; he starts making errors, meekly concedes serve. That their very first match conformed to this pattern may seem surprising, given Nadal's youth and inexperience, but what's also noticeable is that the Spaniard appears older than he is. Federer as a seventeen-year-old looked quite different from Federer as a twenty-two-year-old (and, again, as a twenty-six-year-old). There's a YouTube video of him at seventeen playing Agassi, and the rake-thin teenager is scarcely recognizable: both body and game are nascent, half formed. Nadal at seventeen, though, is very much himself. His game is much as it always would be. His muscles bulge mannishly. Even the image is in place: the long baggy shorts, the sleeveless shirt, the whole sweat-drenched long-haired warrior look. The one difference, in fact, is that the tics aren't nearly so prevalent. Before serving, he only bounces the ball once or twice, and there's little of the anxious self-checking. In comparison to what it would be just a few years later, his disposition seems almost carefree.

Not long after that match, Nadal's ankle played up for the first time, and he missed most of the rest of the season. The pair next met a year later, in the final of the same event. This time Federer, who once again had lost just once so far that year, got his revenge—but only just. Luckily for him, the match was best of five (as all Masters finals were in those days). Nadal won the first two sets and went 4–1 up in the third before Federer finally found his game. He broke back and forced a tiebreak, in which he trailed 3–5 before reeling off four straight points. After that, he cruised to victory.

Over the next couple of years, the same pattern repeated itself. Federer went on dominating the tour, unfussily dispatching all comers—apart from the Spaniard. He set unprecedented heights of excellence and consistency. It began to be said that he was invincible, flawless. Except he wasn't, not quite: the hairline crack was already apparent. After that Miami victory, Federer lost his next five matches to Nadal, all but one of which was on clay, including the semifinals of the 2005 French Open. In the whole of 2006, Federer lost just five times; four of those defeats were to Nadal (the other was to Andy Murray). He did beat Nadal that year in the Wimbledon final (their first meeting on grass) and at the Tennis Masters Cup. But by this point the truth was becoming painfully obvious: Nadal was Federer's nightmare, his bogeyman, his nemesis, the one flaw in his otherwise perfect universe.

3.

All great rivalries are founded on contrast. Federer and Nadal's is no exception. One's a rightie, the other's a leftie. One has a single-handed backhand, the other a two-fister.[1] When the two play, attack meets defense. In any earlier epoch of the game, Federer would almost certainly have been a serve and volleyer; playing in the power baseline era has forced him mainly to stay back, but he's a forward-pressing baseliner who takes the ball early and often comes to the net, increasingly so as his career enters its twilight. Though Nadal's volleys are by no means poor, his preference is to camp out well behind the baseline and use his loopy topspin ground strokes to force opponents to do the same. This isn't to say that he can't also attack to devastating effect, especially with his forehand, which is one of the best the game has ever seen. But Nadal prefers to launch his attacks from a position of impregnability, to put his own affairs in order before going after his opponent. Defense precedes offense; he absorbs, then retaliates. Federer looks to land the heavy blows right away, and defends only if he has to.

As in rallies, so in matches. Federer looks to seize the initiative. His instincts are predatory, domineering. (He is sometimes compared to a leopard or cheetah.) He sets a

---

1. The best tennis rivalries often seem to adhere to this configuration: the same was true of Navratilova/Evert and Borg/McEnroe, although in both cases it was the leftie who had the single-hander.

swift tempo—that unfussy service preparation—and this is
of a piece with his overall strategy, which is to disrupt his
opponent's rhythm, deprive him of time and territory, make
him dance to his tune. After losing to Federer, players often
say words to the effect of: "I didn't feel I was able to play my
game." Nadal's approach is gradualist, incremental. He hangs
back, lies low, lets his opponents come at him. The Spaniard
is sometimes compared to a *capybara*, the buck-toothed
South American rodent, but while it's true that there's a
striking visual resemblance,[2] strategically he's more of a boa
constrictor: instead of swiftly dispatching his victims, he subjects them to a drawn-out asphyxiation.

Because Nadal's instinct isn't to immediately dominate,
because his opponents, at least to start with, often seem
to have the upper hand, his matches have a very different
rhythm to Federer's. They are invariably battles. This helps
explain something I've noticed, which is that his matches
often appear closer than they actually are. Come into the
room while he's playing, and you might assume, from
watching a few points, that it's incredibly tight, or even that
he's losing; then you'll discover that he's actually 6–3, 6–2,
3–1 up. This discrepancy is partly attributable to Nadal's
on-court demeanor—his psychological need to assume the
role of underdog. But it's also connected with his attritional,
counterpunching style, one effect of which is to reduce the
observable gulf between him and his opponents. Nadal's
progress through matches—and through tournaments—is

---

2. For evidence of this, visit capybarasthatlooklikerafaelnadal.tumblr.com

rarely serene. Federer's superiority, by contrast, tends to be plainly in view: even when his matches are tight, he usually seems much the better player.

I suppose another way of saying this is that Federer is—as has often been noted—a kind of aristocrat.[3] He believes in his own superiority, and has no scruples about making others aware of it. There is no part of him that wants to hide his abilities from the world. I am sure that he goes into every match believing that he's better than his opponent, that, all things being equal, he *should* win. As he likes to put it, making the sentiment sound more technical than it is: "It's on my racket." Nadal's the opposite. The dial of his self-esteem is set purposefully low. He goes into every match thinking that only a superhuman effort will result in victory. Like

---

3. Naturally, I mean this figuratively. Nadal and Federer have fairly similar backgrounds: like the majority of tennis players, both are bourgeois. As Elizabeth Wilson points out in *Love Game*, lawn tennis started out as an aristocratic sport—its original setting was the country house—and, during the first half of the twentieth century, it continued to be associated more with idle pleasure-seeking than with bourgeois striving: it migrated to the fleshpots of the Riviera and to California and, in the 1920s, became popular in Weimar Germany. The barriers to entry reinforced its exclusiveness: you had to be independently wealthy to play it to a high level, since the established tournaments were only open to amateurs. (The amateur/professional partition lasted, remarkably, until 1968.) Wilson's overall argument—one I find largely convincing—is that, in recent decades, the sport's original spirit of playful inventiveness has receded. Visually, it has become less like dance and more like boxing. It has become less romantic, more martial. In this context, Federer's aristocratic bearing is significant: it can be seen as another example of his unique era-straddling abilities, his capacity to reconnect the sport with its past. Yet it is somehow typical of Federer that, alongside recalling the old amateur ideal, he also manages to be the consummate modern professional—not to mention the most financially successful tennis player ever.

the small-town boy who stumbles upon the big time, his successes often seem to catch him by surprise. Nadal fans portray their hero as impeccably grounded, while depicting Federer as bigheaded, supercilious. And there may be an element of truth in this. But it's always seemed to me that there's something excessive—almost Uriah Heepish—about Nadal's humility, that, in a way, it's more dishonest than Federer's hauteur, which at least has the virtue of being commensurate with his abilities.

4.

Federer makes playing tennis look supremely easy. He glides, he caresses, he (almost) never stumbles. Though clearly strong, he isn't spectacularly muscled. His body is lithe, sinewy, in proportion. In fact, there's something almost demure about Federer—or a sense, at any rate, that he wears his physicality lightly. He (famously) barely sweats, never grunts, hardly pauses between points, and even punishing rallies don't seem to tax him unduly. He is, as David Foster Wallace put it, "both flesh and not." Nadal's the opposite: he's emphatically corporeal. His body, and its extrusions, are impossible to ignore. He grunts, he sweats, his face contorts, he hurls himself at every ball, he theatrically pumps his fist. In fact, there's something physically unbalanced about Nadal: his arms and thighs seem out of proportion to his torso, and in his memoir he admits that he's unusually clumsy. Unlike Federer, who always appears completely relaxed and poised,

Nadal makes playing tennis look like awkward, stressful work.

All this, no doubt, goes a way to explaining their respective injury records. Nadal, as we've seen, is seriously injury-prone. Federer, throughout his career, has been miraculously injury-free. (A player who floats doesn't put much strain on his body; a corrie-fisted clodhopper is bound to end up knackering his.) But the contrast matters for another reason: it reflects how Nadal and Federer embody opposed ideals of sporting excellence. Everything about Nadal stands for effort and its associated attributes: strength, endurance, courage, determination. Federer embodies the qualities that so often go with effortlessness: skill, talent, elegance, beauty.[4]

There's a division in sport, as in life, between these two sets of virtues. It's not that they can't go together—talented/skillful people can be hardworking, and some would say that

---

4. There's an extent, of course, to which Federer's effortlessness must be illusory. It's not as if he is exempt from the stringent training that all elite-level sport requires. The ease and beauty of his tennis are underpinned by formidable endeavor. Yet that endeavor has never been particularly visible: he has never given the media access to his training blocks, as Murray did in Florida in 2012. He doesn't wear his capacity to train hard as a badge of honor, as many other top players do. And there seems to be some genuine basis to the idea that Federer doesn't have to work as hard as his rivals. As a junior, he was known for never particularly relishing training: his performances were always much better in matches than they were on the practice court. Nor was he subjected to the kind of brutal regime that Uncle Toni foisted upon Nadal: Federer's parents allowed him to make his own decisions about how much he played, what his goals should be. Videos of Federer and Nadal practicing at tournaments suggest that such differences continue: whereas Nadal always practices with extraordinary intensity, Federer, much of the time, simply strokes the ball over the net at half pace, as if he were hitting in the park.

a capacity for hard work is itself a talent—but the human psyche generally leans one way or the other. Some people think, or want to believe, that effort is the key to success; others believe (often despite themselves) that talent is what really counts. People are undoubtedly drawn to talent: when I was at primary school, being "skillful"—like Maradona or Glenn Hoddle—was the highest playground accolade, and I would guess that many more kids today fantasize about being Lionel Messi than Frank Lampard. But life, and its disappointments, have a way of chipping away at people's attachment to talent, of making them acknowledge the worth of the Frank Lampards of this world. For every person who finds unbridled talent enthralling, there's another who mistrusts it, who sees it as "unfair" or dubious in some other way.[5]

What's also true is that in recent decades there has been a marked societal shift away from an attachment to talent and a growing recognition of the importance of effort. Ours is a culture that lays tremendous emphasis on working hard. Being (or appearing) "busy" has become a status symbol: the more you have going on in your life, the more successful and capable it means you are. Various things explain this shift: the free market wants us all to be as productive as possible, and so promotes attitudes and behaviors favorable to this outcome; the rise of antielitism means that talent and skill have become tied in people's minds with unearned privilege.

---

5. And don't the talented have a strange way of living up to such suspicions? The history of sport—football especially—is littered with alcoholic, dishonest, narcissistic, or otherwise unwholesome geniuses, from George Best to Luis Suarez.

(Anyone can work hard, but talent will forever remain the prerogative of the few.) Science has also given a thumbs-up to effort. Many recent accounts of success—both in sport and in other areas—downplay the importance of genes and instead stress the role of practice. For example, the notorious 10,000 hours theory, popularized by Malcolm Gladwell in his book *Outliers*, holds that the prerequisite for excellence in any field is to devote 10,000 hours of practice to it: the Beatles were so good because they spent all that time honing their craft in Hamburg; Bill Gates was a teenage computer geek before personal computers even existed. Other well-known studies trumpeting an antitalent message include Matthew Syed's *Bounce: The Myth of Talent and the Power of Practice* and Geoff Colvin's *Talent Is Overrated.*

But there are also specific reasons why, within sport, effort has come to be so highly prized. Sport in general has become much more professional. The old amateur ideal, which held casual brilliance to be superior to effortful efficacy, has receded. (It had largely disappeared from most sports, including tennis, by the end of the 1980s.) The days when lone geniuses could turn up, hungover and underslept, and lay the field to waste with their blazing talents have long gone, if they ever really existed. Even the superlatively skillful must now bow down at the altar of effort; they, too, must practice endlessly and get themselves in "peak condition." While professionalism has deprived skill of some of its elbow room, it has given a boost to the more Nadalesque virtues. Today's athletes are bigger, more muscled than in the past; they are freakishly fit, capable of competing indefinitely. As if mirroring this, their personalities have become increasingly robotic; practically all sportsmen now speak the same functional language in which effort is depicted as the sole ingredient of success. ("I gave 110 percent, pushed myself to the limit, laid it all on the line," and so on.) Certainly, this is Nadal's attitude in his memoir: when he loses, it's invariably because he hasn't "focused enough"; he must "try harder next time." Significantly, too, he views Federer's ability to ace him repeatedly with naked resentment, as if skill, rather than being something to admire, were an unjustifiable advantage, akin to cheating.

The swing towards effort will never be total. Talent and skill will always have their adherents. And in a strange way, an awareness that talent has lost some of its luster makes those athletes who do rely (or appear to rely) on it—such as Federer—all the more precious. It could be that the shift towards effort simultaneously explains Federer's massive popularity—people love him because they sense he's a dying breed—*and* provides a reason why others dislike him. It also goes some way to explaining why, whenever Federer and Nadal play, so much seems to be at stake. Pundits invariably focus on the question of who will go down as the better player, but in a way this is less important—and less interesting—than the question of which player is ethically superior. Whose attributes are more admirable? Who has the stronger claim on our regard? When Nadal and Federer face one another, more than mere reputation is at stake. Their matches, in a way, are an ongoing dialogue about tennis itself—about how the sport *should* be played, and what its future path might be.

5.

At the time of writing, Federer's record against Nadal stands at 23–11 in the Spaniard's favor. This, it goes without saying, is a dismal statistic—a source of outrage and disbelief. But here we must put our feelings to one side, summon up a semblance of equanimity, and, instead of railing against the situation's awfulness, address ourselves to two tough questions: why has Federer won so infrequently against Nadal? And how much of a blot on his record—on his overall standing as a player—does the failure represent?

In many ways, the first question is easy to answer. It all goes back to Uncle Toni's decision to force his protégé to play left-handed. The bread-and-butter shot of any good tennis player is the crosscourt forehand. Because Nadal's a leftie (albeit not a natural one), his go-to shot is directed at the backhands—and therefore weaker wings—of most opponents. All left-handers have this advantage, although it tends to be offset by the fact that the benefit runs the other way: the rightie also gets to pepper the leftie's backhand. On the other hand, the leftie is used to having his backhand thus peppered; the rightie, who will have mostly faced other righties, isn't.[6]

All things being equal, therefore, a leftie's left-handedness

---

6. The same logic, of course, applies to the serve: the leftie's ability to swing the delivery wide to the rightie's backhand is mirrored by the rightie's ability to do the same to the leftie, except that the leftie will have spent his whole life perfecting that particular serve, and, additionally, will have had ample practice returning serves hit wide to his backhand.

gives him a slight advantage in baseline rallies that might be expected to work in his favor some of the time. With Nadal, however, all is not equal. And that's because his forehand is no ordinary shot but a monstrous spinning, dipping, rearing, kicking thing, a stroke that induces fear and panic in all who face it. The one crumb of comfort most players have is the knowledge that, at least, they have the protection of a double-handed backhand, which, when played well, is, as we've seen, a much more resilient and consistent shot than the single-hander. Facing Nadal's crosscourt forehand armed with a single-hander is, to put it mildly, suboptimal.

Nadal has the best overall win-loss ratio in the open era of men's tennis (it currently stands at .828, a fraction ahead of Borg at .826), and his head-to-head record against other top players is formidable. Basically, before his dramatic dip in form in 2015, no one managed to beat Nadal regularly, with the exception, oddly, of Nicolay Davydenko, who retired from the sport in the autumn of 2014 with a 6–5 record against the Spaniard. Djokovic has got on top of Nadal periodically, most notably in his memorable 2011 season, when he beat him all six times they played, but their head-to-head remains tied at 21–21. Only two current players have a winning record against Nadal: Nick Kyrgios, who beat him in the fourth round at Wimbledon in 2014, and the German-Jamaican oddball Dustin Brown, who has beaten Nadal both times they've played, at Halle in 2014 and at Wimbledon the following year.

Yet a closer look at Nadal's record reveals an interesting nuance: while he beats up on pretty much everyone, against right-handers with single-handed backhands he is especially lethal. There have been a number of outstanding—that is, top ten or twenty—players with single-handers in recent years, and Nadal's record against them makes for painful reading. Against Richard Gasquet—possessor of perhaps the finest backhand in the game—Nadal is 13–1 (the solitary defeat coming in a 2003 Challenger when Nadal retired). Against Stanislas Wawrinka (Gasquet's main rival for that title), he's 14–3 (and one of those losses was in the 2014 Australian Open final, when Nadal's back went into spasm). He leads Tommy Robredo 7–0, Tommy Haas 5–0, Grigor Dimitrov 6–0, Nicolas Almagro 13-1, Philipp Kohlschreiber 12–1.

Nadal habitually annihilates players with single-handers for one basic reason: his deep, powerful, extraordinarily consistent, violently kicking forehand means that he is able to wear them down. Watching on TV doesn't begin to convey the degree of difficulty such players have in countering Nadal's best shot. I have an inkling of the problem from my own experience. Like a lot of tennis players my age, I play my backhand one-handed; and while, ideologically, it's a method I believe in, there are times when I wish I had a two-hander. Up to about low chest height, it's possible to play the single-hander reasonably comfortably, to not have the feeling that your options are being drastically restricted. It's still, relatively speaking, a tricky shot, but at least it can be an effective one. However, once the ball rises that bit higher, when it gets up around your shoulders—as it inevitably does on hard or clay courts against opponents who load the ball with topspin—the prospects of producing a decent shot dwindle dramatically. Physiologically, it's pretty much impossible to hit the single-hander in a consistent fashion, with depth and power, when the ball is up near your eyebrows. And that eventually becomes true for even the best pros as well.

Nadal knows this. He knows that, when he has his opponents where he wants them—playing single-handed backhands at chest height or above—they will find it almost impossible to harm him. They may get the ball back without difficulty, they may catch him out occasionally with a well-aimed shot down the line, they may retreat far back behind the baseline and let the ball drop, or counter the steep bounce by stepping in and taking it on the rise, but, most of the time, they will struggle to gain a clear advantage in the rally. In tennis, if you can repeatedly bring about situations where you know the other person cannot harm you, you have a huge advantage. Winning is as much about neutralizing an opponent's weapons as deploying your own. And that's what Nadal does so successfully, again and again. He does it against all players, of course, but he does it *especially* well against righties with single-handers.

6.

Another factor can be cited in Federer's defense for his terrible record against Nadal. Of the pair's thirty-four meetings, fifteen have been on clay, the surface on which Nadal excels to a quite astonishing degree. Not altogether surprisingly, the Spaniard has won thirteen of those matches. By contrast, just three of their meetings have been on Federer's best surface, grass, and only six on his second best, indoor hard courts. Both on grass and indoors, it's Federer who has the winning record—2–1 and 5–1 respectively. (On the other hand, his record against Nadal on outdoor hard courts is an inexplicably poor 2–8.)

What explains the imbalance in the surfaces their matches have been played on? Various things. The European clay court season—where the top pros play the large majority of their clay court matches—lasts just over two months, from April to early June, but a lot of tournaments are packed in: Nadal, like most top players, tends to take part in five. By contrast, the top pros never play more than two grass court events, and rarely more than three indoors. Despite his injury record, Nadal always seems to be in prime condition for the clay court season: he has only missed it once in his career, in 2004. On the other hand, he regularly misses tournaments towards the end of the year, and doesn't reliably make Wimbledon. In addition, Nadal's performances on grass and indoors are inconsistent: he has frequently been knocked out of events in the early rounds, preventing him from meeting Federer. The Swiss, by contrast, especially during the prime of his career, was a consistent clay court performer: he regularly reached the final of the events he entered, where, invariably, he faced Nadal.

Of course, the distorting impact of surface is only a partial mitigation. A professional tennis player's job is to compete wherever he finds himself playing. And while Federer's 2–13 record against Nadal on clay may be excusable, his record against him on outdoor hard courts isn't. Nonetheless, it is worth pointing out that Nadal has hugely benefitted from playing Federer so often on courts that suit him, and so rarely on ones that don't. Equally, it is worth asking what their head-to-head might look like if the spread had been more even. Projecting from current win-loss ratios, for example, had the pair faced each other an equal number of times on all four surfaces (clay, grass, indoor hard, and outdoor hard), it is possible to calculate that Nadal's lead over Federer would be a *far* more respectable 18–16.[7]

7.

My friend Ben, who once wrote an article explaining why he disliked Federer, has a theory about the Swiss.[8] He thinks he's a bully. When, early in his career, he was easily the best player in the world, he happily trampled over all comers. But against those who have stood up to him—first Nadal, then, to a lesser extent, Djokovic and Murray—his record has been less impressive. Ben says Federer is happy to dole it out, but can't take it. He's a good winner but a poor loser. Like all bullies, he's a coward who lacks true grit, true courage, who

---

7. When they've played on clay and outdoor hard courts, Nadal has an overall winning ratio of .84. On grass and indoors, Federer has a winning ratio of .77. So if the pair played 100 times on clay and outdoor hard, Nadal would win eighty-four times, whereas Federer would win seventy-seven times out of a hundred on the other two surfaces. Combine the two sets of figures, and we can project that, had the pair played 200 times (with an even split between the surfaces), the head-to-head would be 107–93 in Nadal's favor—that is, a winning ratio for the Spaniard of .535. Apply that to the actual number of times they've played—thirty-four—and we get 18.19–15.81 to Nadal, which, rounded, means 18–16.

8. "Disliking Federer," *London Review of Books* blog, July 9, 2012.

preens and flexes and gangs up on the weaklings and then runs off crying when the big boys show up.

Ben additionally says that great champions "find a way," and that, against Nadal, Federer has conspicuously failed to do this. And here, I'll admit, he has a point. Over the years, what has perplexed me most when Federer plays Nadal is how rarely the Swiss has appeared capable of truly battling. Something about playing Nadal seems to reduce Federer, make him indecisive, tactically brittle, even spineless. I have lost count of the number of times their matches have followed the same basic pattern: in the first set, things look good; Federer comes out with an aggressive game plan, and executes it well; he breaks Nadal's serve, looks on top. Then he goes for a bit too much, and misses a key shot, or else Nadal pulls off an extraordinary defensive winner. And from then on, the dynamic changes. Confidence drains from Federer; Nadal becomes pumped up, inspired. Federer starts making unaccountable errors—generally my cue for exiting the room in despair. He may threaten Nadal again, but he never gets back on top. He can't raise his game when he really needs to. In other words, it's their first meeting in Miami all over again.

It's not that, in general, Federer is mentally frail. Despite his reputation for being a front-runner, he can dig his heels in, be gritty and obstinate. He wins an awful lot of matches simply because he plays the big points better than his opponents. Against Nadal, though, such steeliness deserts him. Not always, of course: the pair have had some epic battles over the years—their second meeting in Miami, the 2007 and 2008 Wimbledon finals, the 2009 Australian Open final. In those matches, even when Federer lost, he really fought, and emerged with credit. But there have been too many other occasions, particularly in recent years, when Federer hasn't appeared interested in really fighting Nadal, as if, deep down, he'd resigned himself to losing before the match even started. At times it has seemed as if Federer would prefer to surrender meekly to Nadal than give his all and still come out second best. Mats Wilander once said of Federer—after he'd lost a match to Nadal—that he'd "come out with no balls." Though the phrasing isn't attractive, the sentiment might be right.

What explains this strange capitulatory tendency, so out of character for Federer generally? I've never quite understood it, and nor have I heard anyone else account for it satisfactorily. All I—like anyone else—can do is speculate. And my best shot at a theory is that, at some point, Nadal inflicted an injury to Federer's ego that the Swiss has never fully recovered from. It's important to remember that Nadal has never been afraid of losing to Federer. Early on, he was the underdog anyway, and even now he takes the attitude that Federer, on his day, is naturally a better player than him, that he could lose. Thus, his expectations against the Swiss are carefully managed.

Flip the equation round, however, and it's not the same. Federer, as I've pointed out, is a sporting aristocrat, someone who believes that he's got the shots to win, that victory is "on his racket." And in his early twenties, when he was dominating, there was little to contradict this. Then Nadal came along, and suddenly the situation changed. Here was a player who could soak up Federer's aggressive shots, retrieve balls no one else could, make Federer feel that he had to do something extra to win. For a while, perhaps, this wasn't too disastrous. Nadal may have had Roland Garros, the entire clay court season, sewn up, but Federer was still world No. 1, was still winning at Melbourne, Flushing Meadow, Wimbledon. Couldn't he beat Nadal on grass (as in 2006 and 2007) and, if it really came down to it, fend him off on hard courts, too? That must have been the belief that Federer sustained himself with; and while it remained untested, it was plausible enough. But then, in 2008–2009, the situation changed. Nadal finally conquered Federer at Wimbledon, and, six months after this, almost more devastatingly, beat him in similarly dramatic fashion in the Australian Open final, a defeat that famously prompted Federer to cry. It was as if everything Federer considered his had been taken away from him. He had been overthrown, thoroughly colonized.

In the grand scheme of things, to be deposed in a sporting sense—to go from being the best in the world to being the second-best—may not seem like too dreadful a fate. And Federer, unlike, say, Borg, didn't go to pieces; he hung around, adapted to the reality of post-dethronement life. But much of Federer's career since then has somehow had the air of an aftermath, an anticlimax. It will forever be the case that, when the greatest test came, he wasn't quite up to the challenge. Pundits talk—incessantly, infuriatingly—about the "old Federer," and what they surely mean by this is the Federer who once played with the freedom of knowing that, if he played his best, no one could touch him. That Federer—for all that he has reemerged periodically in recent times—can never be fully recaptured. He is a memory, a chimerical presence. Around 2008 and 2009, the infinite became limited; there was a cruel reduction in scale.

The gravest psychological blows—the ones least easily borne—are those that force a person to change the way he sees himself, that destroy a much-cherished self-image. How exactly Federer coped with those losses to Nadal—how he justified them to himself—is something that only he, and perhaps those closest to him, know. But ever since, Federer has been a different player when he steps on court with Nadal; in some sense, he has been psychologically cowed. And one consequence is that their rivalry, which initially burned so fiercely, has never quite lived up to its promise.

8.

Again, though, in a larger sense, all this could be seen as necessary. The aura of perfection, of godliness, that clung to Federer during his best years needed to be dispelled. It wasn't good for the sport, maybe not good even for Federer himself. Something had to be done, and the gods of tennis duly obliged. Having (presumably) scratched their heads for some time, they sent down the one thing capable of stopping Federer—a bunglesome messenger from a future-gone-wrong, an embodiment of every crudifying technological development of the previous four decades, a player who, with one 4,000-rpm smote of his racket, could smash all Federer's artistry, his subtlety, to pieces. Nadal, one could say, was the price tennis had to pay for Federer's genius.

January–May 2014

In its cleanness and efficiency, there was something unmistakably Federerlike about his rebirth of 2014. In the off-season, he made three announcements: he would be committing to a larger-headed, 97-square-inch racket; Stefan Edberg would be joining him as a part-time coach; and his wife, Mirka, was expecting another baby. He also said that his back was finally better. The desire to start afresh was clearly there—and thankfully his form made it a reality. From his very first appearance in January—at a minor tournament in Brisbane, where he lost in the final to Lleyton Hewitt, and played some enthralling doubles with Nicolas Mahut—there was a spring to his step, a sense of lightness, that hadn't often been in evidence over the previous twelve months.

During these first few months of the year, I watched Federer more avidly, more fervently, than perhaps I ever have. In

the intensity of my scrutiny there was, I think, a new awareness of his fragility. A large part of the shock of the previous
season had been to do with seeing something so apparently
inviolable—Federer's brilliance—rendered so acutely vulnerable. Along with many others, I realized that I mustn't take
it for granted. At the same time, the feeling that he'd pulled
back from a serious crisis imparted a sense of joyousness to
his return. In 2014, Federer seemed a happier, more carefree
figure than ever before. In some odd way, the pressure was
off; being the best was no longer so important. He was happy,
it seemed, to simply enjoy playing while he could. This lightness of spirit affected how I viewed him. It's not that I didn't
care any more; I still desperately wanted him to win. But I
felt less on edge, less bruised by his losses, better able to take
the rough with the smooth.

What made his rejuvenation all the more exciting was that
it was underpinned by a tactical shift. For several years, observers had been urging Federer to come to the net more. In
his prime, he'd been able to beat pretty much everyone playing mainly from the back. But with age, this was becoming
more of a challenge: even if the speed was there, the stamina
was increasingly an issue, especially at Grand Slams. Coming to the net more seemed a logical solution: it would help
shorten the points. How, though, to effect the transition? No
one doubted Federer's volleying ability, only whether regular
net play was a viable option at this stage in the sport's evolution, when the baseline game was so utterly ascendant.

At the Australian Open, however, Federer consciously
pursued a more net-rushing strategy and, rather remarkably,

made a success of it. In the last sixteen against Tsonga, and in the quarters against Murray, he came in far more than usual, but did so with a purposeful unpredictability—occasionally serve and volleying, more often stealing in during a rally. His execution was exemplary—he barely missed a volley in either match—and the strategy visibly foxed his opponents. He swept Tsonga aside in three sets, beat Murray in four (though he should have won in three). In both matches, his ratio of winners to unforced errors was nearly double. There was much talk of the "Edberg effect." So well, so *excitingly*, was Federer playing that I momentarily dropped my guard, and made the mistake of believing that he actually stood a chance in his semifinal against his old nemesis, Nadal. All I can say is that, after all these years, I should have known better than to get my hopes up.

In the months that followed, while Nadal (who injured his back in the final, against Stanislas Wawrinka) stuttered, Federer maintained his excellent form. Early in February, he helped Switzerland beat a Djokovic-less Serbia in the first round of the Davis Cup.[9] He won his first title of the year in Dubai, overcoming Djokovic in the semis with more of the same net-rushing brilliance. He reached the final in Indian Wells, where he lost to Djokovic in a third- set tiebreak. In early April, he propelled Switzerland to victory against Ka-

9. Federer intimated that, health allowing, he would be available for every match of Switzerland's Davis Cup campaign. With Wawrinka in the form of his life, it suddenly seemed as if Switzerland had a genuine shot at winning the competition for the first time ever; their previous best had been a final appearance in 1992.

zakhstan in the Davis Cup quarterfinals and then reached yet another final at Monte Carlo, again beating Djokovic in the semis before losing to Wawrinka.

During these months, it became gratifyingly clear that the Australian Open had not been a one-off, that the "real," albeit modified, Federer was back. The inconsistency and self-doubt of 2013 were gone: Federer was again winning most of his matches easily, and he was competing on level terms with the best. Even the few unexpected losses he suffered during these months—such as to Kei Nishikori in Miami—were "good" losses, the results of understandable fatigue or plain bad luck.

How important was the new racket in all this? Federer himself maintained that the bigger head gave him "easy power" on his serve. But what was also noticeable was that he was getting more consistency and depth with his backhand; the racket seemed to enable him to impart more topspin, enabling him to give himself a higher clearance over the net. And he was volleying better. But there were clearly other factors in his rehabilitation. Having Edberg on his side evidently helped: much as Lendl's belligerence had brought out the best in Murray, so the Swede's coolness seemed to chime with something in Federer. And none of this would have been possible had his back not recovered. Seeing Federer float around the court once again made it clear that he really had been hampered the previous year.

In early May, Mirka gave birth—again to twins (this time boys). In the ensuing weeks, Federer's form—not altogether surprisingly—fractionally dipped: he went out to Jeremy

Chardy in Rome (despite having a match point) and at Roland Garros he lost in the fourth round to the temperamental Latvian Ernests Gulbis. (Again, it was extremely close: but for a poor smash on set point in the second set, Federer would almost certainly have won.) Thankfully, however, the blip was short-lived. When the grass court season arrived, Federer was back to his glorious best, first at Halle and then at Wimbledon. And happily, at both tournaments, I was there to see him.

chapter four

The years between

1.

I should say something about what went on in my life between the cessation of my initial interest in tennis and its subsequent, Federer-inspired rejuvenation. On the whole, this wasn't a happy period. Outwardly, things may have looked fairly normal. I didn't collapse. I went on ticking off most of the conventional milestones—school, university, first job. But in my head, all was misery and confusion. My life was dominated by a protracted identity crisis, and for a long time I was very depressed.

My abandonment of tennis, I should be clear, wasn't the cause of the problem. But it was a symptom of sorts. As I've already suggested, my relationship with sport when I was growing up was tangled, complicated. It was my passion, the thing I was (or believed myself to be) best at. Yet at the same time, I grew to hate the identity it gave me. My family—and my father in particular—laid such stress on intellectual accomplishment that my status as the "sporty one" felt almost laughably inconsequential. The matter was further complicated by the fact that the source of my love for tennis was my father. Since he (it seemed to me) placed sporting prowess well below brainpower in his list of desirable accomplishments, the upshot was a kind of double downgrading: not only was tennis a second-tier interest; it didn't even have the advantage of being wholly my own. I couldn't help but feel that excelling at tennis—or cricket—was a hiding to nothing, since it could only raise me so far in my father's esteem.

Looking back, I suppose the mistake I made was one of excessive literal-mindedness. I grew up thinking that my father's distinctions and hierarchies, the absolute weight he attached to the life of the mind, reflected some wider truth about the world. That's the problem—or one of the problems—with childhood: small things get magnified, what's accidental and contingent becomes cast in bronze. In my mind, my father's views and opinions had godlike authority, and if my experiences didn't accord with them, that must mean my experiences (and not his views and opinions) were at fault. What I failed to understand was how much the dice had been preloaded: for reasons that had nothing to do with me, things within our family had been set up a certain way. It was as if the spoils of my father's personality had, at some formative stage, been shared out between his two eldest children, and while my brother had been handed the most valuable portion, I'd been bequeathed a subsidiary branch.

And so I grew up sure of one thing: that the person I felt myself to be was flawed, insufficient; that I needed to slough him off. The exact identity of this magical alternative being was always somewhat hazy. All I knew was that my chances in life depended on becoming him. Now that I'm a father myself, I find it odd to think that so much of my life should have been given over to this lunatic project of psychic self-immolation. I watch my young son, see how naturally, how happily, he embraces the world, how effortlessly his personality unspools, and I find myself constantly wanting to warn him: be yourself, just be yourself, never try to become what others want you to be. But maybe that's naïve, impossible: I am his father, and the way I see him will inevitably affect how he sees himself; I cannot but influence the person he turns out to be.

2.

My first attempt to become something other than sporty took a fairly conventional form. When I was fourteen, I grew my hair longer, started wearing Doc Martens, took up smoking, and formed a band. In addition to playing sport, I'd always been quite musical. I'd played the piano from the age of six, but had dropped it shortly after we moved to Sussex to make way for guitar. I grappled for a year or two with long nails and contorted hand positions before, in Dylanesque fashion, going electric. An imitation Fender Strat and Marshall amp were acquired; with two friends in my class—both of whom had the decidedly unrock-starlike characteristic of being evangelical Christians—I formed a band. We called ourselves Catastrophe Practice, a name that was borrowed from the title of an early, experimental novel by an old friend of my family's, Nicholas Mosley, whose father, Oswald, had been the subject of my father's first biography. (To this day, I haven't actually read *Catastrophe Practice*, but I still think it's a good name for a band.)

Gigs in our local town were held in a community arts center that had once been a church. The setting—high vaulted ceiling, ivy-bedraggled gravestones—was atmospherically appropriate to the Goth vibe that then predominated. Catastrophe Practice performed there for the first and only time in the summer when I turned fifteen. Alarmingly, more or less our whole school year turned out (there wasn't much to do on a Friday night). My parents came, too, my father clutching his recently acquired, shockingly expensive camcorder, with which he videoed our entire set. Tragically, despite extensive searches, the tape of our performance cannot now be located, and so the authentic Catastrophe Practice sound is forever lost to the world. I do suspect, however, that we would have been considerably better had we had an actual singer—rather than the bassist and I alternately mumbling into the mic— and a drummer who could reliably keep time.

Whatever its musical shortcomings, my performance that night must have made an impression, because I ended up in the arms of Amelia, who went on to become my first serious girlfriend. She was in my year, too, but was older, more sophisticated—she played the flute and read Milan Kundera. She was also quite a bit taller than me. When our relationship began, I came up to her chest. This, inevitably, made kissing awkward: I stood on tiptoes (or on a convenient gravestone); she had to bend.

But this didn't matter, because I was about to embark on my own growth spurt, and in any case we soon graduated to more horizontal modes of congress. Amelia was determined to lose her virginity before her sixteenth birthday. Accordingly, a few months after that first, postgig embrace, we arranged a day trip to London, where we ended up on the sofa bed in my parents' flat, with *Blonde on Blonde* playing on the tape machine. I remember being nervy, reluctant. Actual sex seemed like an impossibly bold step. And I can't say now that I derived that much pleasure from the act itself, beyond feeling immensely relieved that, at least, my worst fear—premature ejaculation—wasn't realized. On the contrary, I was surprised by how long it took: I think we got going around "Leopard Skin Pill Box Hat" and were still at it as the doleful tones of "Sad Eyed Lady of the Lowlands" struck up.

I soon got deflected away from Amelia, rock bands, and other such juvenilia, however. The comprehensive school my brother and I (and, subsequently, our sister) attended didn't have a sixth form, and so the question arose: Where should we do our A levels? The local sixth form colleges were one option, but our father believed that our intellects had already suffered quite enough at the hands of the state school system, and so first my brother, and then I, were guided towards more high-powered alternatives. It emerged that Eton College had a special scholarship, whose purpose was to admit, each year, a small number of state-educated sixteen-year-olds into its sixth form. My brother, whose comprehensive bona fides weren't in fact impeccable (he'd spent three years at a private London day school), took the exam, passed, and duly went to Eton. Three years later, I did the same.

I don't really blame my parents for wanting to send me to Eton. They didn't force the place upon me, and as they saw it, had I not been given the option of going, that might have turned into a source of resentment. All I wish is that I'd known my own mind better, that I'd been able to think clearly and make my own decision, rather than going along with what was expected. The fear of what my father's reaction would be if I decided against going—my sense that he would see it as a personal failing—was strong enough to override all other considerations. It didn't seem to me that I had a real choice. And probably because of this, my time at Eton was unhappy. In the two years I was there, I morphed from the fairly carefree and confident character I'd been at my comp into a frozen, startled being who was unable to show anything of himself to anyone. When others tried to engage me, I wore a rictus smile, said little. And of course, I never told anyone about what was happening. One thing I was certain of was that my suffering would be silent.

What exactly was the problem? Again, looking back, it seems odd that I should have found fitting in at Eton so hard. It's a place that now strikes me as more preposterous than forbidding. Why did I accord it such importance, such respect?

The answer lay in my relentlessly stratified, hierarchical view of the world, which equaled—in fact outstripped—all the considerable efforts the school itself made in that department. Eton was a territory indelibly associated in my mind with beings like my father and brother. It wasn't a place for me. Matters weren't helped by the fact that my brother had made it sound so rarefied. In letters home, he would describe sitting up late with his friends, reading poetry, discussing Henry James. Some of these friends had come to visit, and to me their precocity was extraordinary, alarming. They seemed a different species from my friends at my comp and the prospect of having to walk among them petrified me.

Actually, when I got there, the transition was less shocking than I'd anticipated. The poetry-reading contingent weren't much in evidence. Most people I encountered were fairly normal. Accents aside, the biggest observable difference between my friends at my comp and the boys in my house was the latter's obsession with a form of homoerotic role-playing that involved grabbing each other by the testicles. Even so, the fact that I wasn't intellectually intimidated made little difference. In my mind, Eton had assumed such monolithic proportions, become invested with such daunting grandeur, that I was quite incapable of taking it as I found it. So deeply rooted were my preconceived notions about the place—and my unsuitability for it—that no amount of evidence to the contrary would have altered my behavior.

Before going there, the one thing I'd derived reassurance from was the knowledge that my sportiness would stand me in good stead. Making the first XI at cricket, I was told, would guarantee me school-wide fame and popularity, and might even be a means of getting into "Pop," the elite, colored waistcoat-wearing prefect body. And there seemed little doubt that I was first XI material: after all, I'd been the rising star of my village team, one season achieving a batting average of 526 (a feat that the *Sussex Express* hadn't neglected to mention). Yet here my illusions took a cruel battering. My cricketing prowess didn't translate from the village greens of my boyhood to the playing fields of Eton. I wasn't a complete flop: in my second year, I played for the second XI, and made one or two decent scores. But I wasn't in any danger of being called upon for the jewel in the crown of Eton's sporting calendar, the annual match against Harrow at Lord's. I've never known exactly what the problem was. Maybe it's just that I wasn't as good as I thought; but I've always felt that there was more to it than that, that my failure to excel had something to do with a certain condescension on the part of the school's cricketing authorities. Somehow, I had the sense that my technique—village-honed, a bit irregular—was found to be wanting, lacking in distinction: my left elbow wasn't impeccably high enough, my bat not sufficiently ramrod straight.

Sports at Eton were rationed and seasonally rotated, and because I played cricket in the summer, I couldn't also play tennis, which might have been one way for me to salvage a measure of respectability (not that I was by this point very interested or probably even all that good). Instead I found refuge—in the autumn and winter terms—in a more under-the-radar alternative: squash. It was a game I'd played only sporadically in the past, but now I applied myself to it with grim determination. The familial resemblance to tennis meant that becoming good wasn't difficult; the main requirement, other than being able to strike the ball well, was to be exceptionally fit. I soon made the school team. In the wider Eton universe, this was of little consequence: no one cared about squash. But for me, it was a small vindication, a sop to my pride. I think, too, there was something about the game itself—its repetitive nature; the hemmed-in, boxlike space in which it was played—that fitted with my mood at the time, my sense of having little room for maneuver.

Socially, my time at Eton started badly—in the sense that I made no real friends—and went downhill. My refusal to give anything of myself, I suppose, began to wear on people, especially my housemates. Reticence, which may seem appealingly modest at first, can just as easily become a weakness to exploit. The boys in my house, having initially been well disposed towards me, turned, during the second year I was there, into my persecutors. For a while, they made my life almost unbearable. In this regard, I wasn't unique. At Eton—perhaps as at most boarding schools—it seemed to be the natural order of things for year groups within houses to be stratified in this way, between those who were bait and those who fed upon them. The enforced proximity of boarding-house life—the way we were cooped up each day for hours—made such behavior almost inevitable. The pressure created by the situation had to find an outlet, and the cruelty, in a way, wasn't so much personal as institutional, a flaw woven into the fabric of the system.

My one other compensation during my time at Eton was

work. Somewhat to my surprise, I responded well to the efficiency of the school's time-honed, if often uninspiring, teaching methods, and made swift progress. I worked hard on my essays; they began to be singled out for praise; I developed a reputation for being clever, or even—in the argot of the place—*frightfully* clever. (This didn't contribute to my popularity with my housemates.) I did well in my A levels, and secured a place at Oxford to read English. But in the longer term, this academic vindication proved of dubious benefit. For it stirred my deep-seated belief that my life would be better, all my problems magically sorted, if only I could transform myself into an intellectual; in fact, it gave this fantasy a patina of plausibility. And so, after a gap year mainly spent teaching English in India, I went off to Oxford full of misguided ideas about what I could achieve there, about the sort of person I might yet become.

3.

To begin with, things at Oxford went well enough. I arrived at my college feeling more at ease within myself than I had at Eton, thanks to a recently acquired girlfriend and my Indian gap year. (It's amazing how much difference an ethnic jacket and the ability to roll a joint can make to a nineteen-year-old's self-confidence.) It was also a relief to discover that, while Oxford was by no means diverse, it was considerably less monocultural than Eton. The accents weren't all identical. There were women as well as men!

My college was a sporty place with a largely public-school intake. Its social center was a dingy cellar bar, where groups of rugby lads would sit, downing endless pints, playing raucous drinking games, and, very often, rounding off their revelries by spontaneously exposing their genitals to whomever happened to be in the vicinity. (Nowadays, I doubt such behavior would be tolerated; back in the nineties, it was entirely commonplace.) Not feeling myself to be at home amid such beer-soaked jocularity, I made friends with a group whose inclinations were less raucous. Most nights, we'd sit in one or other of our rooms, drinking, smoking, and chatting—often about the horrors of the bar. I played virtually no sport.

The first real indication that something was wrong came in the summer term of my first year, when two things happened: I caught glandular fever, and I decided to switch from English to history. The glandular fever caused me to be laid up in bed for a few weeks, but I soon recovered. My decision to change subjects, meanwhile, was the product of some typically contorted thinking. I was actually quite enjoying English, and during my first year I'd done reasonably well. It had always been the subject I'd been best at. Changing to history not only meant that I'd effectively wasted a year, but that I now had just two years to complete what would normally be a three-year course. It strikes me now that it was less a decision than a kind of statement, driven by an unconscious desire to please—or perhaps imitate—my father (who, of course, had himself read history). As ever, I was desperately trying to live up to something, to prove that I wasn't some arty flibbertigibbet but a substantial, serious person.

Yet I couldn't get to grips with history at all. The course was drier, more fact-laden than I'd expected. And the teaching—at my college at least—was stodgy and disengaged. I didn't help myself by concentrating on the most inaccessible periods. For some reason, I decided to make twelfth-century Europe my special subject, even though I had no knowledge of the medieval world, nor indeed a great deal of interest in it. The subtleties of ecclesiastical politics eluded me. I struggled to remember the names of the various popes, let alone their contributions to the advancement of the church. A large proportion of my essays remained unwritten.

Nor was I feeling right. Although I thought I'd got over my glandular fever, the feelings of tiredness now returned. Only this wasn't normal tiredness, but a monumental, all-encompassing lethargy that had nothing to do with how much sleep I got. The more time I spent in bed, in fact, the worse it seemed to get. I would wake from unbroken fourteen-hour nights with the vim of someone who'd just completed a 6-mile run. I felt permanently shattered, sucker-punched.

As my work faltered, and my feelings of lethargy intensified, so the rest of my life lost its vigor, its shape. I stopped enjoying Oxford's attractions and became introverted, room-bound. The confidence I'd discovered in my first year vanished. I had one consolation—cooking. I'd developed an interest in this during my gap year, when I'd spent a few months living on my own in London. In my second year at Oxford, I had access to a kitchen, and my days increasingly revolved round planning and executing elaborate meals—sometimes for others, often just for myself. Cooking became the antidote to my tiredness and confusion; it was the one area in which I felt in control. Its role, in other words, wasn't dissimilar from that which sport had once played. It became my lifeline, my escape.

At the end of my second year, I still didn't feel any better. And by now, I was seriously worried about work. I'd arrived at Oxford with a secret fantasy, which was to prove everyone (or at least my father) wrong by triumphing academically. This, of course, meant getting a first. But given how my work was going, such a goal looked increasingly unattainable. My finals were a year away—and there was no way I was going to be ready. I therefore persuaded my college to give me a year off. I went back home to live with my parents, with the aim of recovering my strength and making up the work I'd missed. During that year, I did read a lot of history books, but they merely added to my anxiety and confusion. The more I read, the more I became aware of my own ignorance, how little I—or indeed anyone—could ever truly understand the past. I became preoccupied with the artificiality of history, the (as I saw it) unbridgeable gulf between the authoritative tone required for academic writing and the inevitable flimsiness of any one person's knowledge. Dates and facts swam in my head. It all seemed so arbitrary, so removed from real life.

My energy wasn't returning either. On the contrary, I became more and more morose. Vainly, I sought a cure for my malaise. I immersed myself in the world of alternative medicine: I tried herbal tinctures, acupuncture, meditation, fasting, macrobiotics. But nothing worked. Eventually, with the new year at Oxford fast approaching, I went to my GP, and took up his suggestion (first made a few months earlier) of trying antidepressants. I didn't have any faith that these would help me either—I was convinced that my problems were physical, not mental. But at least they'd be something else to cross off the list. So I was taken aback by the intensity with which they kicked in. Within days of starting my course, I felt an unfamiliar energy coursing through me. My listlessness gave way to jittery excitement. As my physical vigor returned, so my spirits rose. The things that I'd been agonizing about suddenly seemed like irrelevancies. Going back to Oxford would be a cinch.

In reality, however, this buoyed-up state was a snare—hardly better than the torpor that preceded it. During those first few weeks on antidepressants, my confidence scaled ridiculous heights. I thought I could achieve anything, take on anyone. I drank copiously, took large quantities of drugs. One night, climbing about on some rooftops, I lost my footing and fell onto a balcony: it could easily have been worse. Another time, hoping to impress a girl, I smashed up the frontage of a restaurant where I'd once worked as a waiter. (She wasn't nearly as impressed as I'd hoped she would be.) I acquired a new girlfriend—and instantly cheated on her. My behavior was idiotic, unhinged.

Of course, such manic euphoria couldn't last; a crash of some kind was inevitable. It happened a few weeks after my return to Oxford, when I descended into a mood of crippling blackness. The antidepressants I'd been taking no longer seemed to work. And that was pretty much how I spent the rest of my time at Oxford—in a dejected, baffled state. I very nearly left. Yet somehow I did stick with it and—aided by another antidepressant—I made it through my finals, even ending up with a half-decent degree (if not the first I'd so badly wanted). I didn't feel ready to be an adult, but I had no choice. Just like that, I was out in the real world.

4.

A feature of depression—or at least depression as I experienced it—is that it seems to come out of nowhere. It doesn't, of course, but that's the impression it gives. To flourish, it requires you to believe in its impossibility; in some sense you have to consider yourself immune. When I'd been younger, I had never thought for a moment that there could be anything fundamentally wrong with how I viewed myself or the world. My sanity was something I took for granted. And no doubt that's why, when I became depressed, it felt as if something was attacking me from outside, that some evil spirit had entered me, taken over my brain. No doubt this is also why, for so long, I refused to see the problem as anything other than physical. Facing up to the fact that I was someone who got depressed required me to rethink my most basic ideas about who I was.

And yet, by the end of my time at university, it was no longer something I could deny. The evidence was unarguable. I felt awful all the time. This black insidious thing, which seemed attached to nothing, to have no object, was never not with me. In some ways, the worst feeling of all was the sense

of powerlessness it engendered. Because I had so little understanding of what depression was, I felt as if nothing could
possibly be done—ever would be done—to make it go away.

Insofar as I attributed my condition to anything, my
tendency was to lay the blame at the doors of others. I had
a strong sense that I'd been treated badly, that my parents—
and my father, in particular—had overlooked me, not taken
me seriously enough. While there may have been some truth
to this, blame was not a solution. Anger may be one of the
causes of depression, but expressing the anger doesn't rid you
of the problem. The real challenge is to acknowledge your
complicity, face up to the fact that, whatever its origins, your
depression is yours alone, and the solution, however much
you may want it to lie outside you, can only come from
within.

5.

I had little idea what I wanted to do after I left university. I
did not feel (despite my degree) that my prospects of finding
a decent job were good. Inspired by my love of cooking, I
first tried my hand at cheffing. For a few months, I worked
twelve-hour shifts in crowded kitchens, being humiliated by
men twice my age who seemed to take exception not merely
to the way I chopped vegetables but to the very fact that a
"college boy" wanted to work among them. In spite of its
grueling nature, I rather enjoyed the experience. And I regret,
now, that I didn't stick at it longer. As was so often the case, I

lacked the confidence of my convictions. I was worried that
cheffing wasn't a "good-enough" job.

Next, I worked at a company that called itself a "writing consultancy." However, the writing consisted mainly of
replying to letters of complaint on behalf of a major super-
market, which was too disorganized—or too fundamentally
unbothered—to perform the task itself. I wrote thousands of
such letters, becoming a master of the empty phrases that are
the stock-in-trade of corporate communication. ("We have
carefully investigated the matter and we assure you that we
will take every step possible to remedy the problem to your
satisfaction.") That job, too, quickly lost its appeal.

What I actually needed, more than a job, was help;
and eventually—and very luckily—I found it. My mother,
though no particular fan of therapy herself, had been urging
me to try it for some time. Through a friend, she obtained the
number of a psychoanalyst. And so, one day, I found myself
knocking on the side door of a large house in North London.
The woman who greeted me was in her forties; she had oddly
formal manners, a German-sounding name, and an accent I
couldn't place. I ignored the couch, and sat opposite her on
a leather armchair. In that first session, she didn't strike me
as hugely sympathetic. She seemed more interested in discussing the practicalities of future meetings—which hadn't
even been arranged yet—than in finding out what my problems were. This struck me as presumptuous. What insight,
I thought, could this woman—whose life was evidently so
disconnected from my own—possibly have into my psyche?
The session ended, and I didn't return.

This realization led to another: tangled up as it had been with questions of family and identity, my love of sport had never had the chance to express itself fully. This feeling of incompleteness applied in particular to tennis, the sport I'd loved first, and which had been most affected by my relationship with my father. My swift abandonment of it in my early teens now struck me as a cause for regret. After all, I'd been pretty good.

My job presented me with an opportunity—and, in a way, an incentive—to dust off my old Wilson Ultra and get back on court. In May 2006, I went to the Hay literary festival with some colleagues, where, I learned, the annual writers versus publishers' tennis match was taking place. I offered my services, and ended up turning out for the publishers, who were a player short. My game was inevitably rusty—I'd played only a handful of times in the previous decade—but was otherwise intact: I could still come over the ball with my single-handed backhand; I had decent volleys, a probing forehand. I won my first match, a singles, against the event's organizer—a thriller writer in his fifties who had elegant strokes but was a sluggish mover—and then teamed up in the doubles with the obvious star of the show (in both the sporting and literary senses), the flamboyant, long-haired owner of an independent publishing house. Together, we thrashed a poet and another novelist, giving overall victory to the publishers. We were presented with a surprisingly large silver trophy, which, for some reason, was entrusted to me. I was told to return it in time for next year's match; I'm ashamed to say I failed to do this and to this day it sits on the "trophy shelf" next to my desk.

After this, word must have spread among London's tennis-playing literati that there was a new competitor on the scene, because I started regularly receiving emails from writers, both obscure and relatively famous, asking me if I'd be up for a game. Thus my job—which largely consisted of persuading writers to review books—and my leisure interests neatly began to dovetail. I could respond to a novelist's request for a game by pinging back a suggestion of a book for him to review. An email asking for nine hundred words on the new Hilary Mantel novel might be appended with a confirmation that tomorrow's match was still on. My tennis assignations often ate into work time, but this didn't bother me unduly, since I could plausibly argue that they helped me to carry out what was in any case a vital part of my job—forging contacts in the literary world. Instead of treating contributors to lavish lunches, I could meet them in the park for a couple of brisk sets. I even considered filing expenses claims for the cost of my court bookings and tennis balls.

Thanks to all this, I became aware of something I hadn't fully appreciated before, which is that an unexpectedly large number of writers are mad about tennis. David Foster Wallace wasn't alone. I suppose this isn't really so surprising, when you consider the affinities between the two activities. Writers sit at home all day, and can keep whatever hours they choose, so have plenty of opportunities not just to watch the sport (an especially realizable goal in the age of satellite TV and online streaming) but also to go out and play. A game of tennis is in many ways the perfect way to break up a writing day. Unlike, say, cricket, it doesn't take up too much time, nor does it require much organization. Early afternoon, when inspiration often flags, tends to be the best time to play tennis: this is when the courts are most likely to be available (and cheapest), the weather at its most amenable. A tennis match between two writers is also a chance, during the knock-up, and at changeovers, to exchange gossip and discuss works-in-progress. The result is that tennis can come to seem like a natural—indeed vital—extension of the writing life.

But the similarities run deeper. Tennis, like writing, is technically complex: all those strokes to master, all those rules to obey (don't take the racket back beyond your shoulder when volleying; assume the trophy pose just before striking the serve). It's a game of endless small adjustments, a sport for tinkerers, perfectionists. At the same time, tennis is an unusually—perhaps uniquely—psychological sport. It's not just that players have to be good readers of character, able to figure out what an opponent's weaknesses are and how to exploit them, it's also that the sport itself exerts such acute mental pressures. The margins between success and failure are so tiny, both at the micro and macro levels. (A difference of a quarter of an inch in your swing can make the difference between a winner or a miss; just one or two points can decide the outcome of the match.) This is why, playing tennis, it's so easy to get frustrated. At every level, it's common to encounter players who, more than anything, resemble madmen: gesticulating, hurling their rackets, talking to themselves. No sport is more inward-looking than tennis, more conducive to emotional turmoil, downward-spiraling patterns of thought. And in this, too, of course, it has something in common with writing.

7.

After a while, most of the writers I played dropped off the roster for one reason or another: we lived too far away from one another, or I beat them too easily. (Here I would like to say "or vice versa," but actually this was rarely the case: let's just say, first, that I tended to have a significant age advantage and, second, that literary types aren't always the most natural of athletes.) My regular partners dwindled to a few. One was the long-haired publisher from Hay, whom I used to play on the indoor courts round the corner from his West London house, always at the (to me) painfully early hour of 8 a.m. The publisher, who never seemed to sleep—he would fire off emails at five in the morning, as well as regaling me with tales of his late-night exploits—had clearly been a good player in his youth, and was still useful. He had a solid defensive back-court game, but his biggest weapon was a wickedly spinning serve (he was a leftie), which, when he got it just right on the ad side, would snake its way into the side netting before I could lay a racket on the ball. We were fairly evenly matched, but he seemed to win more often than me. Afterwards, over a smoothie, he would tell me about the books he was planning to publish, every one of which would be "amazing," "path-breaking," "sensational." (No one could accuse him of not championing his authors.)

My two other regular opponents at the time were both novelists: one an unprolific Indian with a lazily wristy, almost disdainful style, who at one point had been a regular hitting partner of Martin Amis's; the other a tall Englishman whose game was awkward and inelegant but doggedly effective. The Indian was the more talented player but, unlike the unflappable Englishman, had an uneven temperament. Whenever things weren't going his way, he would berate himself remorselessly: "No no. Don't doooooo that! For Christ's sake!" He also had a habit, when matches got tight, of resorting to what is widely regarded as the lowest tactic in tennis: the moon ball. On a few occasions, he beat me after employing this strategy, and afterwards he would be even more racked by self-hatred than usual. "I just can't bear how I played," he would say. "All those slow loopy shots. It's terrible." I always thought this a tad disingenuous: if you're going to play (and win) in a certain way, then at least don't disown the tactic afterwards. It was as if he wanted to rise above himself, to care less than he did, yet was powerless to prevent his true competitiveness coming through.

8.

I soon discovered that I had demons of my own. When I'd played as a boy, I'd been a shouter, a racket thrower.[1] Now, in adulthood, the problem resurfaced. Except that, in a way, things were worse this time round, for not only did I no

---

1. Federer, famously, suffered from serious anger problems, too, both as a junior and when he first joined the tour. He worked with a sports psychologist when he was sixteen and seventeen and became much calmer.

longer have the excuse of being young, I also had more reason than ever to feel frustrated. The problem was that I just couldn't find my game. In 2008, after moving from North to South London, I joined a club and began to play with a wider—and better—circle of people. The whole process was incredibly frustrating. I would lose to players I should have beaten, only just beat people I should have wiped the floor with. (At least, that's how I saw it.) Tennis, admittedly, is a hard sport to pick up after a long layoff—much harder, in my experience, than cricket or squash—but the problem went beyond mere rustiness. At root, it was psychological. I simply couldn't handle the pressure of playing close matches. In, say, a casual doubles, my game would be fine, but then, when I played singles, it would rapidly deteriorate. My arm would become tense; I'd start patting the ball back. And of course, this would make me angry. I'd scream and yell, rage against the fact that I couldn't play as I wanted to—as, deep down, I knew I could. And all this self-haranguing would, inevitably, cause my level to drop further still. My wife (then girlfriend) once saw me play a match, and professed herself mildly perturbed by the tormented, endlessly self-critical person I became.

The result was that I hit a wall. I was a decent player, but not a really good one. I couldn't consistently perform when it mattered. I played for my club's second team, but wasn't winning a lot of matches. I felt that, rather than improving, I was going backwards. This went on for quite a while, and my sense of frustration grew. At one point, I even thought about giving up playing tennis for a second time.

The breakthrough came in the form of a book. One day, a colleague at work, himself a tennis fan, asked me if I'd ever read *The Inner Game of Tennis*. I hadn't heard of it. A couple of days later, it appeared on my desk. The book, first published in 1974, was by a Harvard English major turned tennis coach named Timothy Gallwey. It was, I discovered, a gripping read. (When first published, it had been a bestseller.) Gallwey's central contention—in itself provocative—is that by far the most important factor when it comes to improving your tennis is what goes on in your head. Get the "inner game" right, he says, and there is virtually no limit to how much better you can become.

Central to his argument is the idea that, when we play tennis (or any sport), we have two selves: Self 1 and Self 2. Self 1 is conscious and rational, the part of the brain interested in instructions, in critical thinking. It's the "teller." Self 2 is the largely unconscious part that performs tasks— like hitting a ball—automatically, unthinkingly. It's the "doer." The problem most tennis players have, says Gallwey, is that they ascribe too much importance, too much power, to Self 1. That self has its uses—for example, it's indispensable if you need to work out how to travel from one side of a city to another—but its usefulness when it comes to tennis is limited. Self 2 really runs the show. The game, after all, takes place at a speed that rules out conscious decision-making. When the ball comes towards you, you don't have time to reflect on what shot you are going to play; you just have to play it. Similarly, hitting the ball is such a complex operation (all those different body parts moving together) that it has to take place of its own accord, through a near-instantaneous process of brain-to-body signaling. Yet, Gallwey points out, most players talk to themselves as if Self 1 were in charge. When something goes wrong—when they hit a shot out, or make a poor decision—they bring in Self 1 to try and fix it. "Don't do that! You can play much better!"

Such an approach may seem logical; we're used to relying on Self 1 to solve problems. But in tennis, Self 1's critical outlook is of no assistance. You can't "think" yourself into playing better any more than you can think yourself into sleeping more deeply. Moreover, trying to solve the problem this way interferes with Self 2, which can't get on with doing what it does if it's constantly being harangued by Self 1. The more Self 1 criticizes and blames, the more impeded Self 2 becomes: muscles get tighter, movements become jerky. You play worse, and Self 2 gets (wrongly) blamed for it.

The trick to reversing this negative spiral, according to Gallwey, is to learn to shut Self 1 off entirely—to learn to play without "ego involvement." Instead of giving in to the temptation to criticize yourself, you should observe your play—good and bad—nonjudgmentally. During rallies, he suggests disengaging the mind by focusing intently on the seams of the ball. Between points (and, in tennis, there is a lot of time when you're not actually playing), he advises visualizing the shots you would ideally like to play. Self 2 must be trusted, allowed to run the show. As the repository of your tennis wisdom, it will know how to fix things when you're not playing well. Only if it's unimpeded will it enable you to play your best.

When I first read *The Inner Game*, I was intrigued but skeptical. I have never much trusted the self-help genre, and some of Gallwey's language was off-putting. There's a fair bit of seventies mumbo-jumbo (talk of "higher consciousness," etc.) and, not surprisingly, the book seems dated (he speaks at one point of Stan Smith's serve being an ideal model for men, and Billie Jean King's for women, as if a woman can't imitate a man, or vice versa). Moreover, he makes some over-the-top claims. I was particularly struck by the absurdity of one passage, for example, in which he describes how, thanks to the inner game, he was able to start returning serve standing just a foot behind the service line. If the tactic were adopted by the pros, he says, it could start a "minor revolution in the game of tennis, reversing the long-standing advantage of the server."

(For years, I was convinced that this passage offered evidence that Gallwey, for all his brilliance, was also pretty bonkers. "Just tell that to John Isner's opponents," I wanted to say. But these days I'm not so sure. After all, in the summer of 2015, didn't Federer himself start deploying the exact same tactic, his so-called SABR move, to devastating effect? Gallwey, in fact, may have been a prophet.)

Yet I recognized Gallwey's portrait of the endlessly self-critical, Self 1–dominated player: after all, it described me perfectly. And I was struck by his description of how much we take Self 2 for granted. It's pretty remarkable, after all, that we can play tennis at all: just to intercept a small, fast-moving object and hit it roughly where we want to, and do so repeatedly, is a cause for wonder. Even our bad shots are remarkable. The book's message, in a way, is simply this: give yourself a break. Value what you are able to do naturally. I found this pertinent.

In 2009, I began trying to utilize Gallwey's "inner game." It wasn't easy to turn off Self 1, but when I managed to do it, the benefits were dramatic. The breakthrough came when I took on Chris, a player at my club who perennially topped the ladder. I'd played him a couple of times, and he had beaten me easily. I didn't think I had a chance. And to start with, the pattern was familiar: he was his usual consistent self; I made mistakes; my serve went awry; I frequently double-faulted. But, making a big effort, I resisted the temptation to harangue myself. I managed to quieten the voices in my head, and instead focused on simply playing—on the ball crossing the net, on the feel of the racket in my hand. And something suddenly changed. My level began to improve. Soon I was staying with Chris, not making my usual errors, hitting shots that surprised me: clean winners from the back of the courts, hard angled first serves that set up forehand putaways. For the first time in ages on a tennis court, I felt wholly calm, undistracted. It wasn't just a question of locating the game I already knew I possessed. It was better than that. I was discovering that I was capable of more than I'd ever realized.

Halle, Thursday, June 12, 2014

1.

If you're a Federer fan—indeed, any kind of tennis fan—my advice would be this: get yourself to Halle. It beats Queen's and the O2 arena by a mile. It beats Wimbledon. In fact, it's hard to imagine a tournament more carefully calibrated to the needs—the *pleasures*—of those who attend it. Yes, the Gerry Weber Open—to give the event its proper title—is the Big Rock Candy Mountain of tennis tournaments.[2] The

_____

2. Gerry Weber, it turns out, is Germany's answer to Philip Green, and Halle is the birthplace of the Gerry Weber fashion empire. The town, as I discovered, is inordinately keen to remind you of these facts.

tickets are cheap, and they're readily available. The beer flows plentifully, and isn't remotely watery. The food is fantastic (although I wouldn't recommend it to vegetarians). The tennis is great: when I went, much of it was spellbinding. Moreover—and this, too, was a considerable bonus as far as I was concerned—there almost certainly won't be any English people there. The one downside is that it's a bit of a schlep to get to.

My decision to go was somewhat last minute. My wife, a criminal barrister, works long and unpredictable hours, and most mornings and evenings I have to be around to help with the child care. This can make trips abroad—or even long days out—hard to arrange. In June, my wife's schedule was particularly onerous: for several weeks she was booked to do back-to-back trials. Although I was hardly in a position to complain, I was worried about what this might imply for my Federer-viewing habits. An overseas trip seemed out of the question.

Then, in mid-June, a trial my wife was embarking upon, in which she was required to defend a particularly vicious-sounding pedophile, collapsed. Suddenly, she had a week off. Halle had just got underway, and I realized that this break in my wife's work presented me with an opportunity. If I went, I'd be guaranteed some serious up-close Federer watching—and who knows, perhaps I might even get a chance to meet him? I didn't contact the press department. My attempts to get accredited to other tournaments hadn't been terribly successful. Insofar as I was a journalist, I was really only a literary journalist; any kudos I'd built up in that area didn't transfer to the world of tennis. In any case, I rather liked the idea of traveling to Halle as a normal fan. So I dialed the number for the tournament's box office. To my surprise, a friendly woman who spoke English picked up the phone, and told me that there were still tickets available for all four remaining days. For what seemed a remarkably modest sum—just over £100—I booked myself a "multi-day package." (If only obtaining tickets for Wimbledon, or indeed Queen's, were so simple!) Then I booked myself a flight to Hanover—one of three large cities in the general vicinity of Halle.[3]

On Wednesday evening, I caught my flight, and stayed the night at a Holiday Inn near the airport. Next day, I set off for Halle by train. Federer was due on court for his first match of the tournament at 1 p.m.; my plan was to arrive in good time, giving me a chance to settle into my hotel and look around. Unfortunately, the trains were behaving in a most un-Germanic manner: there was some kind of technical glitch, and the operator was running a reduced schedule. My journey was delayed by a couple of hours, and I ended up having to travel the last twenty-five miles by taxi.

At just after 1 p.m., I was deposited at the Gerry Weber Sportpark, a sprawling complex of halls, gyms, hotels, and stadia situated on the outskirts of Halle. (My hotel was a ten-minute walk away, in the center of town, but, in order

3. Halle, Westphalia—where the tennis takes place—should not be confused with the much larger town of the same name in East Germany. I initially made this mistake, and came perilously close to booking myself a flight to Halle-Leipzig.

not to miss anything, I decided to check in later.) I quickly made my way to the Gerry Weber Stadium—an impressively large, vertiginous structure with upper and lower tiers and a retractable roof. I took my seat—sadly in the upper tier. The players were knocking up.

Federer's opponent was world No. 44, João Sousa, the Portuguese No. 1 and, according to some, the best Portuguese player of all time (which says more about Portugal's standing as a tennis nation than Sousa's merits as a player). In theory, the match should have been a doddle for Federer— yet it was anything but. In the first set, he wasn't playing terribly, but he was regularly finding the net with his forehand, especially when stretched wide. (This particular shot, I always think, tends to be a barometer of how well he is playing.) The set went to a tiebreak, Federer made a few uncharacteristic errors, and suddenly he faced two set points. He managed to save them, one with an outrageous crosscourt forehand winner, but Sousa—who was playing really astutely—kept the pressure on and prevailed 10–8.

At this point, I began to feel mildly sick. Having come all this way specifically to see Federer, it seemed a distinct possibility that he would suffer one of the most calamitous losses of his entire career. What would I do then? Catch the first plane home? It was a reminder, among other things, of how merciless professional tennis can be. Federer hadn't done anything grievously wrong; he just wasn't at his best. This was understandable, given that it was his first match of the year on grass. (Sousa had already made it through a round.) Yet if this minor dip in form resulted in defeat, it would be perceived as wholly unacceptable. The narrative would instantly be reframed: rather than marking a glorious return, the first few months of the year would be seen as a blip, masking a larger story of terminal decline.

Fortunately, Federer got his act together. After a nervy start to the second set, he broke Sousa in the seventh game. The main difference now was that he was timing his cross-court forehands, giving him vital leverage in baseline rallies. With minimal fuss, he served out the set, then quickly broke at the start of the third, bringing up his opportunity with a delicious in-out forehand dink. By now his tennis was carefree and teasing; there was a sense that he had his opponent on a string. The mood of the crowd changed from anxious to appreciative. Federer cantered through the final set, serving four aces in one game.

2.

Halle, as I said, is great if you like eating (and I *really* like eating; in fact, it may be second only to watching Federer in my list of favorite activities). Stepping outside the arena after Federer's victory, I was stunned by the number of food and drink stalls. They seemed to stretch in an unbroken ring round the entire stadium. Halle is not a big tournament—there are only two courts—and yet there was easily more food on offer than at the whole of Wimbledon. Nor was it by any means all beer and sausages. I saw people tucking into plates of creamy pasta, pizzas topped with crème fraîche (a speciality of Alsace). There were plump prawns and fish frying on a barbecue, grilled steaks and pork chops, pancakes, ice cream, bowls of strawberries dunked in red wine. The choice was paralyzing. Where to begin?

Eventually, I queued up in front of a stall specializing in various iterations of pig on bread. There was cured ham, salami, and a third substance that looked suspiciously like raw minced pork. Could it really be? Would that even be *legal?* The woman behind the counter didn't speak English and, when I enquired as to what it was, she simply replied: "*Mett.*" Intrigued, I ordered one. And indeed it *was* raw minced pork, unadorned but for a few slivers of raw onion. Banishing from my mind all thoughts of tapeworm (surely it *must* be safe; all those Germans couldn't be wrong), I ate my *Mett* and, surprisingly, found it really quite tasty—like a rustic steak tartare. For a moment, I flirted with the idea of ordering another, but then thought better of it, and settled instead for a salted herring sandwich.

3.

Back in the arena, Rafael Nadal, the top seed, was up against the eccentric, dreadlocked German-Jamaican Dustin Brown. I was curious to see how Nadal would fare on this court, which looked considerably faster than the ones at Wimbledon—much closer, in fact, to an old-fashioned grass court. The Spaniard had won the French Open—for the millionth time—just a few days earlier. Usually, he skipped the Wimbledon warm-up events entirely, but he'd decided to play at Halle this year because, having suffered early losses at Wimbledon the two previous years, he wanted more time to adjust to the grass.

But Nadal wasn't destined to get the practice he was seeking. Brown, ranked 85 in the world, batted him aside in an hour. From 4–4 in the first set, the German went on a rampage that saw him reel off seven consecutive games. I'd seen Brown play a few years earlier at Queen's, and I knew he could be unpredictable. But I had no idea he could be *this* unpredictable. For those seven games, some mad spirit of genius entered him, and the shots he produced were truly surreal—125 mph second-serve aces, sneaky sideways-spun drop volleys, service returns that streaked to the corners for winners, jubilant slam dunks. Even when the Spaniard got up in the rally, Brown contrived ways to win: early in the second set, he hit two of the best on-the-run backhand lobs I've ever seen.

Nadal was helpless; he could barely get his racket on the ball. As the match wore on, the crowd—which had been pretty animated when Federer was playing—became positively demented. Brown himself was leaping about all over the place, tossing balls (or sometimes his racket) high in the air, reveling in the sheer lunacy of it all. A defeat for the Spaniard, of course, meant that the tournament wouldn't get the Nadal–Federer final its organizers must have been hoping for. The pair hadn't met on grass since 2008; a rematch (especially on this court) would have been fascinating. But in truth, I wasn't bothered. Watching Nadal being thrashed was just such *fun*.

In the afternoon's final match, Federer reemerged, this time to play doubles, partnering his childhood friend Marco Chiudinelli. Federer, of course, is an amazing doubles player—he just doesn't get to do it very often—and I was excited to have the chance to watch him. From the start, he dominated proceedings: his interceptions were blindingly fast, his pickups effortless. The match was over pretty quickly.

Afterwards, the atmosphere outside had turned festive. A band was performing German-language renditions of classic rock songs. Everyone was necking beer, guzzling food. I strolled around for a while, taking it all in, snacking on a *Wurst* here, a *Nackensteak* there. I was totally on my own—there were no other British people about—and yet I felt strangely at home. It was something to do with the out-of-the-wayness of the setting, how entirely removed it was from my normal life. Because there was no possibility of my fitting in, I didn't feel any pressure to do so. I could simply enjoy myself, a solitary (and slightly unsteady) observer. When it began to get dark, I made my way to my hotel. Halle's streets were completely deserted—was the whole town at the tennis? In my room, I fell on my bed, and switched on the TV. It was the opening day of the World Cup. Brazil were playing Croatia. I watched for a while—and saw Neymar score a couple of goals—before falling asleep.

Halle, Friday,
June 13, 2014

1.

On my second day in Halle, I only saw Federer practicing. He was slated to play his quarterfinal against the Taiwanese player Yen-Hsun Lu, but at the last moment Lu dropped out with a back injury. News spread, though, that Federer was having a practice session on the other court. I was a bit late getting there—pretty much everyone from the main stadium had already decamped to the far smaller Court No 1, desperate for a glimpse of the player they'd come to see. There were long queues outside; getting a seat was out of the question.

Instead, I climbed up a wall (a friendly man gave me a leggie), dragged myself up by my hands, and, craning my neck, peered over the top of one of the stands. (There were lots of other people doing this; I had to do some nudging to get myself a place.) And thus, for a few delicious minutes, I got a glimpse of what must be one of the most enjoyable sights in tennis: a fully relaxed Federer playing a practice match (or, more accurately, a practice tiebreak). I didn't recognize his opponent; someone told me that he was a local German player, a doubles specialist. By any normal measure, he was phenomenally good, but Federer made him look like someone dragged in from a local park. He hit winners at will. Drop shots, carved from behind the baseline, landed an inch or so over the net. Whether he stayed back or served and volleyed, it made no difference: his opponent couldn't win a point.

2.

Despite Federer's nonappearance that day, the tennis didn't lack for excitement. In fact, one of the matches was truly remarkable—among the most dramatic I've ever seen. Dustin Brown, fresh from his conquest of Nadal, was playing the German No. 2, Philipp Kohlschreiber, a dead ringer for the Chelsea defender John Terry. Brown, at first, couldn't recapture his form of the previous afternoon, and Kohlschreiber eased into a one-set lead. Then, just like that, the magic sparked up again: there was the same improbable stroke play, the same delirious leaping about (and a near-identical crowd reaction: everyone, it seemed, wanted "Dreddy" to win). In what felt like minutes, Brown had opened up a 5–0 lead. Then, just as quickly, his inspiration deserted him and, in a torrent of wild thrashes and double faults, he handed his opponent the next five games. At which point—abracadabra!—the brilliance reemerged, and he broke serve to win the second set.

Kohlschreiber must by now have been completely disconcerted. It is normal for players to have hot and cold spells, but Brown's swings were off the charts. What on earth was he going to do next? Just about anything seemed possible. But what he did, in fact, was what was least expected: he knuckled down. The match became a dogfight, a test of concentration, of will. The third set went to a tiebreak, and that tiebreak, like overnourished dough, expanded beyond its intended limits, became a bloated, distended thing. It went on and on; the score kept rising; both players refused to budge. At 15–14, on his fifth match point, Brown had his best opportunity: a forehand that sat up, begging to be hit. (He belted it long; a few days later, when I interviewed him, he described it as a shot he'd make "eight out of ten" in practice.) At 16–16, Brown, at the net, had a high easy ball, and went for a backhand slam dunk, a shot he'd been making all afternoon—but this one caught the net. Next point, he hit another easy forehand long. Kohlschreiber had won 18–16: for many tennis lovers, an evocative score line.

3.

I also had my first encounter with the Backpack Babes that day. I was hanging out by the entrance to the stadium, which also happens to be where Roger-Federer-Allee begins. It's called a road, but in truth it's more of a driveway, leading the 55 or so yards from the stadium entrance to the Gerry Weber Sportspark Hotel, a luxurious, five-star establishment where the players and their entourages are put up. During the tournament, at least, Roger-Federer-Allee is barred to civilians; when I tried to walk down it, a thick-necked security guard swiftly moved to block my progress. The walkway has borne its current moniker for a couple of years; before that, it was Stichstrasse (named, presumably, after Michael Stich). The rechristening took place at a special ceremony attended by the town's mayor, tournament director Ralph Weber (son of Gerry) and, of course, Federer himself—who described having a street named after him as "kind of surreal." (How Michael Stich felt about it is not on public record.)

There I was, hoping that maybe—just maybe—Federer himself would appear, taking what would, I supposed, be an eponymous constitutional. My plan was to collar him and tell him about the book I was writing, at which point—inevitably—he would invite me back to his hotel for a coffee to discuss it further, and he and I would saunter together down Roger-Federer-Allee, past the astonished, now fawning security guard . . . (OK, OK, I was actually just planning on asking for his autograph.) But Federer didn't show up. Instead Sabine Lisicki did—she pulled up in a car with blacked-out windows, and rushed past, clasping half a dozen rackets. (I didn't get her autograph either.) A little while after this, a group of eight or so, mainly middle-aged women, all with identical red and white *RF* backpacks, appeared and began posing for photos—backs to the camera—under the Roger-Federe-Allee sign. In addition to their backpacks, most were wearing *RF*-branded hats, jackets, and trainers; a couple had donned chunky *RF* earrings; several had dyed red hair. I got talking to Margo, a Dutch woman in her fifties, who told me that they'd all met in the forums on Federer's website and that they frequently traveled together to tournaments around the world. Margo, who was less festooned with regalia than the others, seemed mildly embarrassed by the backpacks. "It's just a bit of harmless fun," she said.

Margo and I chatted for a while about our mutual love of "Roger." (In hardcore fan circles, it's always "Roger.") Like me, Margo had first seen him play in 2003—at Rotterdam—but unlike with me, the entrancement had been instantaneous. "I am a massive tennis fan in general," she told me. "I have always loved the game and I like other players, too. But as soon as I saw Roger, I knew he was different." Her reasons for adoring him were much the same as mine. "It's his beautiful style, that's the main thing. His single-handed backhand. I have always liked that style of playing. I don't like the modern power game. I grew up loving people like Maria Bueno and Bjorn Borg." Margo said that she had seen Federer four times at Wimbledon, every time queuing up overnight. "I've even met him a few times," she added. "He's so friendly. He always comes and talks to us when he can. That's why we adore him."

4.

That night, once the tennis was over, the partying started up again. Another band performed—this time with a female singer who was apparently a big pop star in Germany. I again did my rounds of the snack stalls and the beer stands, eliciting mainly friendly, sometimes quizzical, glances, having the odd fragmentary conversation. Later, on my way to the hotel, I went by a slightly different route, and discovered the one place in the town where there was some vestige of life—a bar on the corner of the main square. Inside, the World Cup was being shown on a big screen. The holders, Spain, were playing Holland. Spain—who had been pretty much unbeaten for a decade—were of course the favorites, but the match turned into an Orange rout. Once the Dutch got going, they kept on scoring, and eventually triumphed 5–1. It felt like Brown versus Nadal all over again, the arrogant Spanish getting their comeuppance at the hands of the swashbuckling underdogs. (And while the atmosphere in the bar wasn't anything like as febrile as in the stadium, there was quite a bit of pro-Dutch cheering.)

By the end of the match, I was pretty drunk, and a little bit euphoric, which may explain my amusement at discovering, in the men's toilets, a vending machine offering three products: a "Mini Vibrator," a pack of condoms labeled with a crudely drawn phallus, and a "Travel Pussy," whose strapline read: "*Die Künstliche Vagina.*" It struck me as being like some descending roll call of possibility, a sad delineation of a German man's night: absurd optimism (the mini vibrator) giving way to vague hopefulness (the condoms) before the final, grudging acceptance of the inevitable (the Travel Pussy). *Künstliche*, I later learned, means "artificial" in German, but at first what I thought was being offered was a cuntlike vagina—which would have been a truly baffling proposition. Yet in a way, this vending machine struck me as consolingly symbolic, for it confirmed to me something that I'd already been feeling, which is that Germany—or maybe just this part of Germany—was a curiously easygoing place, where being friendless somehow didn't matter, where it was acceptable— perhaps even expected—for unlucky men to trudge back to their bedrooms and take refuge in the comforts of a three- euro Travel Pussy.

In this mood—light-headed, a bit dislocated—I headed back to my own hotel room (without, I hasten to add, any vending machine products).

chapter five

The greatest match

1.

It was one of the worst days of my life. Although a few other things—being dumped, losing an unborn child—have been more painful, in tennis terms, certainly, no day has been more harrowing. That gusty, rain-sodden Sunday, the agony got going just after two thirty and proceeded to unfurl across the afternoon, bleeding into twilight and dusk, gathering in intensity as it went. Finally, in the pixelated gloom, with suspension imminent, the diurnal span exhausted, a netted forehand settled the matter. Yet this conclusion, far from bringing relief, left only a battered, numbed despondency.

I watched it all with my then girlfriend (now wife) in the

first-floor room that would become our son's bedroom. In those days, my girlfriend shared the house with her mother, and the room was used as a den, or snug. Shoebox-shaped and thickly carpeted, it had a wall-mounted TV on one side and a patterned cream sofa on the other. This sofa was exceptionally capacious and soft: a sofa for sinking into, for hunkering down upon. The room itself was a haven, a place to retreat to for four-o'clock snoozes, for tray-supported suppers in front of bad movies. But that afternoon, it was anything but consoling. For nearly seven hours, it became a torture chamber.

Some great tennis matches pop up out of nowhere, catch their audiences—and their participants—by surprise. Pancho Gonzalez's first round epic against Charlie Pasarell at Wimbledon in 1969 was one such encounter; John Isner versus Nicolas Mahut in 2010 was another. That the 2008 final proved special was a shock to nobody. Its classic status was virtually preordained. The players were competing not just for the Wimbledon crown but for the No. 1 ranking, which Federer had held continually for four and a half years, but which he was virtually guaranteed to relinquish if he lost. Nadal was seeking his first Grand Slam victory on a surface other than clay. If he won, he would be the first man since Bjorn Borg in 1980 to win both Roland Garros and Wimbledon in the same year. If Federer won, it would be his sixth straight Wimbledon, eclipsing the record of five straight wins he shared with Bjorn Borg. (Actually, William Renshaw had won the title six times on the bounce in the 1880s, but no one paid attention to that.)

At the same time, Federer was looking to avenge his humiliating defeat by Nadal at Roland Garros four weeks earlier, when the Spaniard had triumphed for the loss of just four games. Over the previous three years, Federer and Nadal had faced each other in every French Open and Wimbledon final: Nadal had won on all three occasions in Paris; Federer had prevailed both times in London. Symmetry demanded a Federer victory, but there was no denying which way the scales were tilting. Each Nadal win in Paris had been more comprehensive than the last; Federer's wins in London were becoming more difficult. The previous year's final—itself a classic—had gone to five sets, with Nadal squandering break-point chances early in the fifth. And Federer's form coming into the championships had been patchy. He'd lost (to Novak Djokovic) in the semis in Australia and his spring hard-court run had been disrupted by glandular fever. He'd won two titles all year—his most meager pre-Wimbledon return since 2002. The general feeling, reflected in many pundits' predictions, was that regicide was in the air.

Even before the match, the parallels with 1980—previously regarded as Wimbledon's most epic final—were apparent. That year, a cool, undemonstrative right-hander had sought to capture the record for most consecutive Wimbledon titles in the modern era by defeating a passionate left-handed upstart. Borg had managed to see McEnroe off, but the following year, when the American beat him, such was Borg's chagrin that he soon quit the sport. If the Spaniard won, would Federer do something similar? And of course, the comparisons became even more pertinent during the match, which not only equaled 1980 in brilliance and drama but featured, like the earlier encounter, an unbearably dramatic fourth-set tiebreak.

In one sense, however, history didn't repeat itself. The usurper, and not the champion, won.

2.

What I remember most to begin with are the squandered opportunities. He kept on getting break points and failing to convert them. This had been a problem in the past against Nadal: in the 2007 final at Roland Garros, he'd won just one of seventeen such chances. Now a similar pattern asserted itself. Three slipped from his grasp in the opening set: one in the fourth game (with Nadal already a break up), another two with the Spaniard serving at 5–4. The first two of these points were weirdly similar: both times, he got himself in a good position, hit aggressive down-the-line backhands, shaped to come to the net, and then thought better of it. The hesitations were so slight as to be virtually imperceptible; at the time, I'm not sure I noticed them. But McEnroe, commentating for NBC, remarked that Federer had twice "gone against his instinct." But for these small moments of doubt, Mac suggested, he would probably have won both points.

Early in the second set, Federer finally managed to break Nadal's serve, and raced to a 4–1 lead. He was by now playing at his best, cantering through his service games (as he had all tournament), regularly finding the target with his favorite in-out forehand—a particularly lethal shot on grass. But then, serving at 4–2, 30–30, the shot betrayed him: he got his footwork slightly wrong and blasted a midcourt ball into the tramlines. Perhaps not coincidentally, Nadal had, earlier in the game, pulled off a devastating forehand pass. Was this still in Federer's mind when he hit his shot at 30–30, making him think he needed to do something extra? Probably. The miss gave Nadal a break point, which—inevitably—he took. Federer's break advantage was gone.

Yet he kept on pressing. In the next game, from 30–0 down, some superb defensive play helped him engineer another break point. Nadal directed his first serve to Federer's forehand—a surprise tactic—and Federer dumped it into the net. With Federer serving at 4–4, the skies darkened and the wind visibly picked up. The drag and curve on the ball became extreme; the players continually had to make last-ditch adjustments to their shots. Federer, downwind at the Royal Box end, missed a couple of first serves, was tentative on a couple of backhands, got broken again.

The game that followed, with Nadal serving for the set at 5–4, was one of the best of the match. Despite the conditions, both players raised their games. Federer took the lead with a stunning diving volley; a winning serve gave Nadal the next point and he then went 30–15 up with a booming down-the-line forehand. Federer responded with a deep backhand return and a wrong-footing forehand volley that died on the grass. By now the Spaniard's service preparations were becoming increasingly laborious. At 30–30, with the wind swirling, the sun moving in and out of the clouds, he embarked on a ball-bouncing sequence that threatened to become interminable. After twenty or so bounces, Pascal Maria, the umpire, announced a code violation. ("Not now! I mean, come on!" McEnroe objected.) Nadal barely reacted. When the point got underway, the Spaniard again found himself under the cosh: Federer, skipping to his left, crunched a forehand deep to his opponent's backhand and ghosted into the net. But now Nadal's remarkable defensive capabilities revealed themselves. Sensing that Federer was moving in, but was doing so from a slightly leftward position, Nadal opted not to drive his backhand but to float a delicate chip to the opposite service box—the one area of the court Federer couldn't cover. It was a shot of real brilliance, and it brought up set point.

But Federer wasn't done yet. On the next point, he hit a backhand crosscourt slice of his own, the angle catching Nadal out. At deuce, the wind came to Federer's aid: as Nadal was about to unleash a forehand, the ball lurched violently and he ended up pushing it into the tramlines. On break point, Federer did everything right: he hit a perfect return, then an angled crosscourt forehand, forced Nadal out wide, came to the net . . . But still it wasn't enough. Nadal, fully extended to his right, hammered his backhand down the line; Federer, lunging to his left, could only feebly parry his volley back. The Swiss player retreated, and duly lost the point. He flung his left arm into the air, as if to say—I can't play any better, and still the ball comes back! A minute or so later, Nadal had won the set.

3.

By this point, of course, my mood had turned sour. The atmosphere in our little box room had become funereal. Watching Federer lose is never an experience I enjoy, but it's particularly despair-inducing when he loses to Nadal. And it all seems much worse if the match is close. A full-on massacre—as had occurred at the French Open a month earlier—at least has the virtue of clarity, of swiftness. Yet here, there was endless scope for regret: if only Federer had taken just a couple of his chances, played the big points that bit better. Had he been playing badly, even that might have provided grounds for optimism; at least then there would be the prospect of improvement. But Federer was at his best, and was still being beaten. The prognosis was dire, incredibly bleak.

In the third set, maddeningly, it happened again. The earning—and losing—of break points continued. There were two in the fourth game, another *four* in the sixth game. Such outlandish profligacy, such ridiculous waste! And once again, the margins were so tiny. In the fourth game, there was a shot of Federer's that was called out, and which he refrained from challenging—although replays showed that it had clipped the line. A few points later, Nadal challenged a shot of Federer's that looked plumb on the line, but turned out to be an inch or so out. ("That may well be the best challenge in Wimbledon history," McEnroe noted.) Either one of those points could have turned things round, given Federer the grip on the match he so desperately needed. But it was clear to me somehow that his luck had been cursed, that the gods of tennis had—for whatever reason—decreed a Nadal victory.

Federer, unsurprisingly, was becoming tetchy, agitated. Whereas in the first two sets the mask of serenity had rarely slipped, now shards of anger regularly broke through. There were repeated arm flaps, shouts of "*Nein,*" shakes of the head, and rolls of the eyes. (For Federer, such gestures are tantamount to a full-blown tantrum.) The skies were rapidly darkening now—rain was imminent—and so, visibly, was the defending champion's mood.

Then, serving at 3–3, Federer played a couple of clumsy points and found himself 0–40 down. Surely this was it. It was unthinkable that Nadal wouldn't win the game and, from there, go on to claim the match. After all, *he* hadn't been squandering his opportunities. (So far, he'd converted three break points from four, compared to Federer's one from twelve.) I was resigned to the awful inevitability of what was happening: a match that had promised so much was going to fizzle out pathetically; just a month after his Parisian thrashing, Federer was going to lose in straight sets *again*. Except that now, shockingly, Nadal tightened up. On the first break point, he missed a tricky backhand. On the second, he framed a wide first serve. On the third, he hit a second serve to his forehand into the net. Three errors, none glaring, but all, in the circumstances, surprising. Federer, with a shout of "Come on!" unfussily wrapped up the game.

Five minutes later, the rain came. The players were gone for nearly ninety minutes. Today I have almost no memory of this interval, but my wife tells me that I went into the

garden, picked lots of rocket, and made some kind of impro-
vised pesto, which we ate with pasta. I can well imagine the
frantic need for distraction that would have driven me into
the kitchen. For the match to be suspended, left hanging
like that: how agonizing that must have been. I would have
known, objectively, that Federer's chances were minimal, but
equally there would have been a small irrational voice within
me telling me that the odds might still be overturned. After
all, nothing had been conclusively decided: Federer was still
in this; Nadal *had* missed those break points.

According to legend, when Federer left the court, he was
intercepted outside the locker room door by his then girlfriend (now wife), Mirka Vavrinec, who subjected him to a
haranguing in which, among other things, she reminded him
that he was "Roger Federer, five times champion," and that it
was time to show this to the world. The American journalist
L. Jon Wertheim reported that, in response to this public
dressing-down, Federer "nodded sheepishly."

When the match resumed, Federer appeared galvanized.
The set went to a tiebreak, and he now raised his game
magnificently. His first three serves—all to Nadal's forehand
wing—were aces. Then, with two lacerating forehands, he
broke consecutively to go 5–2 up. Nadal, as ever, rallied
strongly and pulled the score back to 5–6. Federer now had
a serve to close out the set. Before stepping up to the line,
he asked the ball boy for a towel—something he hardly ever
does. He then paused for a few seconds while the chants of
the crowd died down, and as he did so the cameras caught
the quick hard stare he shot down the court at his opponent.

Yet again, his serve was perfect: the ball cascaded to the outer edge of the service box and was past Nadal almost before he moved. I remember, at this point, feeling a new kind of admiration for Federer. He was making a contest of this, displaying guts. Even if he didn't win the match, at least he was going to go down fighting.

4.

Matches as good as the 2008 final, with their constant ebbs and flows, their frequent minicrises, are the product, in part, of tennis's eccentric scoring system. In a tennis match, everything is provisional until the final shot is played. Out-and-out dominance can swiftly disintegrate; seemingly unassailable leads can be overturned; even the most apparently inconsequential passage of play can suddenly assume the status of high drama. The ingenuity of the system is the way it breaks up the basic, repetitive action of tennis—the playing of points, one after another—so that what might otherwise seem predictable is imbued with uncertainty, a teasing sense of ranged possibilities.

The system could easily have been different. In the 1860s and 1870s, when lawn tennis was first developed as a more strenuous alternative to croquet, there were several versions of the sport. It was often played on nonrectangular courts; the scoring tended to be based on rackets (a precursor of squash), with games consisting of 15 points, or "aces"; the height of the net varied considerably (early on, the nets were sometimes as high as in badminton). When the first tennis clubs began to appear in the 1870s, attempts to codify the sport were inevitable. In 1875, the Marylebone Cricket Club (which then acted as self-appointed overlord of the nation's sporting affairs and functioned as the game's governing body) formulated the first set of official rules: the cumulative scoring system of rackets was to be adopted; courts were to be hourglass shaped; players were only allowed one serve. Fortunately, two years later, when the All England Croquet and Lawn Tennis Club decided to stage the first-ever lawn tennis tournament at Wimbledon, it rebelled against the MCC, and adopted its own set of rules, based on the 15–30–40-game progression of real tennis. (It also opted for rectangular courts and second serves.) The All England Club's version of the sport quickly became the standard one and, with surprisingly few modifications, is what is still played today.

Why was it such a good thing that the All England Club version prevailed? For a start, tennis's scoring system gives the game its aura of singularity, of romance. No other sport (apart from real tennis, which nowadays is pretty obscure) follows the 15–30–40 progression for determining the outcome of games. No one quite knows how the system originated. Various theories exist: that it in some way mimics the progress of a clock (although why in that case 40 and not 45?); that it's to do with stakes in gambling; that it refers to the physical progress up a court in some primal French (or even Italian) version of the game. But none of these has ever been proven.

Of course, if some strict rationalist were to take over tennis, he or she might decree that, instead of 15–30–40, etc., games should be the first to four. After all, that is basically what a game is: a first-to-four contest (with the requirement of a two-point advantage). But that would be to miss the point of the system, whose cleverness lies precisely in its non-literality. When one starts a game in tennis, one doesn't think: I need to get to four. One thinks: I've got to win this game. The effect is to remove linearity from the equation and make the winning of a game seem more physical than numerical; the sense the player has is of moving through prescribed stages. This feeling is intensified when the score gets to deuce, at which point there's a marked sense of advancing and retreating, of being stuck in a place you want desperately to break free of.

Why this matters is that it serves to detach the smallest unit of tennis—the rally—from any notion of accumulation. A point is merely a stepping stone to something greater: winning a game. And a game is itself a means to a further goal—winning a set—which, in turn, is a means to winning the match. In a sport like basketball (about the most straightforwardly accumulative sport possible and, perhaps not coincidentally, American in origin), the relationship between any individual play and the final outcome is obvious: if one team scores a basket, it will boost their points tally, making them more likely to win. But in tennis, point and final outcome are separated from one another both by the cryptic terminology and the tripartite buffering of game, set, and match. You can win more points than your opponent, win more games, and still come out the loser. A certain indirection is thus built into tennis: each layer of action (point, game, set) yields to the next, and all, finally, are encapsulated within the whole that is the match.

All this relates to something often noted about tennis, which is that not all stages of a match are equally important. The sense of pressure continually shifts. A game point (particularly if it's a break point) matters more than a 15–15 point; a game at the end of a set matters more than one at the beginning; a deciding set matters more than a first set; and so on, until one arrives at the most critical juncture of all, match point, which, you could say, is the only point in tennis that *truly* matters, since it's the only one that's essential to victory. Yet the real beauty of the system is that these shifts are themselves indeterminate: although, during a match, you sense that certain moments are especially important, you have no way of knowing just how important they really are until the match reaches its conclusion. Knowledge is suspended until the final reckoning. For example, how vital were those three break points that Federer saved from 0–40 in the third set of the 2008 final? At the end of the third and fourth sets, they appeared absolutely crucial. At the end of the actual match, perhaps not so much.

Not surprisingly, because of its distinctive rhythm, tennis has often been likened to other things. In *Love Game*, her idiosyncratic history of the sport, Elizabeth Wilson suggests that tennis is a uniquely erotic game, and sees the scoring system as being integral to this. Just as the rally enacts the basic pattern of desire, the players pressing with "stroke after stroke" before building to the "final unanswerable shot," so, she says, the scoring system produces a further erotic undertow, with its guarantee of regular "climaxes and anti-climaxes." Others have seen the rhythmic thrust of tennis as mimicking life itself. The novelist and critic Geoff Dyer captured this well in an article about the 2010 Isner–Mahut epic, when he wrote of how the match—which lasted two and a half days—became a kind of existential drama, a meaningless (and, presumably, distinctly unerotic) battle to keep "non-existence at bay." In a telling phrase, Dyer wrote of how, in a tennis match (as in life), "sudden death and perpetual extension are inextricably paired."[1] What both Wilson and Dyer depicted, from very differing standpoints, was how the tennis scoring system forces a focus on endings, on the frequent little deaths—points of nonexistence—that occur throughout a match, and which foreshadow the point of arrival/termination that is their culmination. Whether ecstatic or eliminatory, life-affirming or life-obliterating, the *end* in tennis is very much the thing.

5.

For a tennis match (or any sporting contest) to be great, various elements have to be present: superlative skill; twists and turns; moments of nerve-shredding tension; all this occurring within the context of a fierce rivalry; the occasion itself being one that really matters. While all these were there in 2008, the match had another ingredient—a sense of newness, of

---

1. "The epic deadlock of the south-western front," *Guardian*, June 24, 2010.

unfamiliarity. And what was unfamiliar about it was mainly to do with Federer, and the way that, as the match progressed, he found himself operating from such an unusual position. Suddenly his superiority, which had always seemed so secure, so inviolable, was being urgently called into question. Even on grass, Nadal, it seemed, was capable of matching, perhaps bettering, him. What was Federer going to do—what was he *capable* of doing—about it? That became the real question.

One thing was clear: Nadal wasn't going to back down. Extreme pressure was what he thrived on. Warriorlike in appearance and mentality, his whole life had been a preparation for this moment. Therefore, if Federer was going to hang on to his title, he was going to have to draw on something that lay beyond mere talent, mere skill: some reservoir of resolve within himself, a core of pure will.

As the afternoon wore on, the contest acquired a flavor that was not only different from how it had been at its start, but was also unlike any of the pair's previous encounters. When, in the past, Federer and Nadal had played at Wimbledon, the focus had generally been on Nadal: Did he have the skill to beat Federer on grass? That question had been resolved—in the affirmative—by the first two sets. So the proposition was now inverted: Did Federer have the fortitude, the courage, to get the better of Nadal? Instead of Nadal needing to become more Federerlike, Federer needed to out-Nadal Nadal.

This sense of role reversal was reflected in another shift: it was now Nadal who was creating the chances. From 3–3 in the third set, Federer earned just one more break point in the match; Nadal, by contrast, earned another nine. (The final tally for both players was thirteen.) Federer was now regularly finding himself under intense pressure. Serving to stay in the match at 4–5 in the fourth set, he lost the first two points of the game, both to inspired play by Nadal, before somehow battling through the next four points (three of them with second serves). At 5–6, an errant forehand cost him the first point of the game, and he came perilously close to losing the second when a Nadal forehand missed the line by a whisker. Again, Federer made it through. In the ensuing tiebreak, he recovered from 2–5 down before saving match points at both 6–7 and 7–8. Through all this, there was a sense—again novel for Federer—that he was clinging on by his fingertips. His life, certainly, hadn't been a preparation for this, but in the circumstances he had no other option. And I was impressed, as well as moved, to see how valiantly he embraced this role. Extreme adversity was bringing out the best in him.

As had been the case in 1980, the fourth-set tiebreak was the match's defining moment, the distillation of its essence. In some ways, it was unfortunate that this ghostly precursor existed, because it lent an inevitable air of paltriness to the 10–8 score line, a sense of coitus interruptus, of excitement prematurely cut off. While the 1980 tiebreak had spanned thirty-four points, prompting the Isner–Mahut question—when will this end?—the 2008 edition was more of a crash-and-burn affair. It reached its apogee around the 7–7 mark and from there had nowhere else to go.

At 7–7, with Federer serving, Nadal played the first of the two shots for which the tiebreak is famous: a down-the-line forehand on the run that seemed, a fraction of a second before he hit it, impossible. As with most of Nadal's best shots, the disbelief was occasioned not so much by the shot itself as by the fact that he got to the ball at all. Federer's forehand approach was excellent: it was flat and pacey, craftily angled. Nadal appeared out of the rally. Yet the Spaniard's secret— the voodoo quality that makes him unlike any other tennis player—is that when time is lacking, *he speeds up*. Like some jet-powered superhero, he acquires extra gears. Drawing now on this reserve of explosiveness, he hurtled across the baseline and shoveled the ball past Federer at the net.

On the next point—match point down, receiving serve— Federer produced a passing shot that was no less stunning, and likewise seemed a summation of his gifts. It was a backhand struck, on the run, from his left-hand corner, a (sort of) reverse image of the winner that preceded it. The difference between the two largely lay in the two players' movement. Whereas, prior to his shot, Nadal appeared to quicken, Federer, before his, seemed to slow down. As the ball approached him, there he was, already waiting for it, and the resulting stroke—a caress down the line—had an unhurried, casual air. The shot produced the cognitive dissonance so often associated with watching Federer: the confusion of seeing the extraordinarily difficult made to look easy.

Great athletes often interact with their environments in distinctive ways. This is true of both Nadal and Federer. Nadal's special ability is one of self-transformation; when the ball isn't there, he speeds up to meet it. Federer's is the opposite: he makes the ball—or, one could say, the universe—slow down, bends it to his own stately pace. Perhaps this is finally what really divides them: one transforms himself to fit his environment; the other makes his environment fit him.

In those two points, with their sense of parry and riposte, it seemed as if the whole match—the entire rivalry—had been pared back to its essentials. In a sense, the match could have ended right there; nothing else was really needed. But of course, the scoreboard's demands had not been satisfied. Neither player had got to three sets. When Federer won the next two points, arrival at that terminus was once again deferred.

6.

By now I felt exhausted, enfeebled, tremulous. The match had already gone on for longer than seemed possible. How much more drama could it conceivably contain? And yet things were—inevitably—about to crank up again. The fifth set began evenly, a bit sedately. In the first few games, both men played cagily, as if readying themselves for what lay ahead. For the first time in the match, the tennis seemed flat, devoid of inspiration; there were as many errors—a forehand that Federer missed completely, a couple of mistimed backhands from Nadal—as winners. In the fifth game, with Federer serving, it began to rain. Play was halted, at Federer's request, with the score on deuce. It was just after ten to eight. It wasn't clear whether there would be time to finish the match that evening. If the delay was anything other than brief, play would have to be adjourned till the following day. Secretly, I hoped this would happen. Although ordinarily

Federer would be the player with the momentum, having recovered rather than surrendered a two-set lead, in this instance, it seemed to me, the opposite might be the case. Losing the fourth set, failing to take his chances, would, if anything, increase Nadal's determination. A fresh resumption, a clean dash to the finish, might just favor Federer.

But it was not to be. The rain clouds blew over and at twenty past eight the players returned. Federer wrapped up the game with two aces (a good sign) and then, five minutes later, with Nadal serving at 3–4, created his one clear chance to win. A forehand winner got him to 30–40: his first break point of the set, his final one of the match. This time he didn't fluff his opportunity but Nadal stood firm, immovable. He hit a 124-mph serve down the middle and, off Federer's only marginally short return, smashed a forehand down the line that the Swiss, at full stretch, could only lob up weakly. Nadal closed out the point with an on-the-bounce smash. On Nadal's next service game, Federer got to 30–30—another sniff—but again, Nadal shut him out with two swinging first serves backed up by forehand winners.

Throughout his career, Nadal has always been at his most dangerous when on the rack; he has the jujitsulike quality of being able to draw strength from his opponents, to feed off their own good play. Around this point, with Federer pressing, Nadal became visibly more energetic, more focused; his shots became heavier, his grunts louder, the glances he directed towards his entourage more determined. Remarkably, the overall quality of the tennis rose. Both men were now striking the ball with exceptional intent. My only clear memory of those final few games is of the endless break points Federer had to save. By now I was close to meltdown; I remember at one point writhing around on the floor. Increasingly, I had the feeling that this couldn't go on any longer, not only for the obvious practical reason—because the light was deteriorating—but because emotionally, dramatically, it *had* to end: I—we—couldn't stand it anymore.

Our little room was by now almost dark. The match had entered a new, and almost certainly decisive, phase, a tortuous end game. There was a magnificence to Federer's resistance; he kept on sending down aces, hitting winners. Surely it was futile. Although who knew? Perhaps if this carried on long enough, if he saved enough break points, enough match points, Nadal would crack and Federer would clamber out the other side. But finally, at 7–7, he faltered. His game didn't collapse; he simply got his feet wrong on a couple of forehands, the type of shots he'd been making all afternoon. It was understandable, after so long, and with the court now so dark, that such small misjudgments should creep into his game. Still he fought: he saved another three break points, one with an ace, another with a serve that Nadal barely touched. But the fourth time round, his best shot let him down once more when, approaching the net, he skewed a forehand long. He had been broken. Nadal would serve for the match.

There was one more bit of drama—one more agonizing death throe. Match point down, in response to a wide Nadal first serve, Federer produced a crosscourt backhand that was virtually a clean winner—his best return of the entire match.

But Nadal brought up match point again, and this time Federer dragged a simple forehand into the net. An anticlimactic finale. As he would say afterwards: "I could barely see my opponent." Nadal, after a celebratory writhe on the grass, a quick half embrace at the net, clambered up over the commentary box—presenting his groin to McEnroe as he did so—and into the players' box directly above it. In those days, the players' teams sat pressed together, one in front of the other. As Federer was the higher-ranked player, his team occupied the front row, which meant that Nadal had to reach over the front seats to embrace his entourage, including a (finally) smiling Uncle Toni. As he did so, the camera caught Federer's father, Robert, standing aside, warmly clapping. In order to come back down—by a different, less hazardous route—Nadal had to walk along the top of the commentary box, past the rest of Federer's team. Federer's mother, Lynette, was also clapping, as was his agent, Tony Godsick, who helped Nadal as he climbed down. Mirka, however, was notable for her lack of animation. As Nadal walked past, she sat staring straight ahead of her, the expression on her face stony, blank.

Federer, meanwhile, was sitting in his chair, packing up his bag. He'd put on his cardigan: a cream number emblazoned with gold *RF*s. He looked lonely—and a bit silly. Watching again now, I am struck by how young he looks. He was twenty-six, and still fresh-faced. But his days of greatness—of being king—were over.

Halle, Saturday, June 14, 2014

1.

On my third day in Halle, I managed to get media accreditation. Though I'd come to see Federer, it struck me that the story of the tournament so far was Brown. True, he'd been knocked out in the quarters, but he'd beaten the world No. 1, come tantalizingly close to beating Kohlschreiber, and he'd played some scintillating tennis. He was still in the doubles (facing Federer and Chiudinelli) and so would be around for at least another day. With his unusual mixed heritage and camper van backstory, he was also, it seemed to me, an intriguing character.

My plan was straightforward: if I could persuade someone—a newspaper, a magazine—to let me interview him, that would get me into the press box. And if I got into the press box—well, then I'd be in a much better position to capitalize on any opportunities that arose to get close to Federer. Who knew, maybe I could even swing an interview with him? Surely, at this out-of-the-way tournament, my prospects of getting the all-important (but so far elusive) "access" would be better than practically anywhere else.

The first part of my plan went smoothly. I fired off emails, proposing an interview with Dustin Brown, and got a positive response from a Sunday paper. I went to the press desk, and got myself accredited. ("Next time, Mr. Skidelsky, perhaps you should consider letting us have your request *before* the start of the tournament.") I was in—but into what, exactly? I'd had a vision of the press room as a gilded place where delicious victuals would be on offer and where grizzled correspondents would stride purposefully about, swapping recollections of long-forgotten players ("D'ya remember Koolykonikosis? Small wiry guy? Weird backhand?"). No doubt, too, the pros themselves would frequently drop by and engage the journalists in brisk badinage. ("Hey, Chris, what do you mean, I wasn't at my best? Screw you!")

So the reality was something of a letdown. The press box was a utilitarian space with indifferent food, a total absence of players, and newsmen who, far from being the larger-than-life characters of my imagination, were mostly a bunch of grim-faced hacks from obscure regional papers. In fact, I only encountered two people who were remotely friendly: a student from Düsseldorf, who was covering the event for his university radio station; and a man from Bangalore, who talked vaguely of being the tennis writer for a "leading sports website" but who I came to suspect was even more of a blagger than me. His name was Dinesh, and he was traveling around Europe, covering the clay- and grass-court seasons; he'd been to Rome and Paris, and was hoping to go to Wimbledon—although, like me, he'd been refused accreditation. He, too, was seeking the holy grail: an interview with Federer. Dinesh had intense, staring eyes and a habit of leaning in too close when talking. No sooner did we meet than he began pressing me urgently on whether I had any tips on "getting to Roger."

I told him that I was having little luck in that department myself. While the tournament's media representatives were friendly and helpful, they were decidedly downbeat whenever the conversation came round to the Swiss. Getting access to anyone else was eminently possible: they set me up with a one-on-one with Brown; I was told I could speak to Kei Nishikori, to Alejandro Falla, to Philipp Kohlschreiber. But Federer—well, that was almost certainly out of the question. I asked politely, did my best to be charming, and they said they'd look into it—though whether they did I have no idea. Certainly nothing resembling a positive answer came back. Federer, it seemed, was unavailable.

But I could attend his press conference, which was scheduled later that day—after he'd played his singles and doubles semifinals.

2.

Nishikori, Federer's singles opponent, promised to be a test. The young Japanese player had beaten him twice before; their matches were always close. If Federer didn't raise his game from the previous round, I could see him going out. But in the event, he didn't have much trouble. From the start, he played as if he knew exactly what he wanted to do. He didn't blast Nishikori off the court, but rather brought him to heel with tempered aggression.

The seats reserved for the press corps were reasonably good ones (my new status had facilitated a descent from the upper tier), and what struck me now—although no doubt this was partly due to Nishikori's scrawniness—was how physically imposing Federer is. One doesn't necessarily think of him this way: he isn't tall for a tennis player, nor particularly bulky. But he radiates a sense of heft. His physical presence is very different from that of his rivals. Nadal, for instance, is defined by his musculature; his biceps and thigh muscles protrude almost pornographically from his sleeves and shorts. Djokovic is a human spider: insubstantial of torso, all the force, the emphasis, of his body resides in those sprawling, tentacular limbs. But with Federer, what you notice most are his shoulders and chest—they are the source from which his power emanates. Of course, he has lots of other, contrasting physical attributes: he's lithe and catlike, light on his feet, fiendishly quick. But it's all underpinned by a core of solidity that seems to be located in his solar plexus.

Federer won the first set and continued to boss Nishikori in the second, though he did let slip a break advantage. He was serve and volleying more now, bounding to the net, punctuating the points with exuberantly punched volleys: all good signs for Wimbledon. It had rained just before the match and, to the strains of "Raindrops Keep Falling on my Head" (and while a man wearing a bear jumpsuit leapt about on the grass), the roof had been unfurled. But the skies soon cleared and the roof had been retracted, and now a lemony midafternoon sunlight cascaded into the stadium. The thought came to me, suddenly, that life was pretty good. Here I was, in this unfamiliar place, a glass of beer in my hand, watching Federer playing well. This conjunction of circumstances aroused a feeling of contentment. I felt as if all was OK with the universe.

The crowd, I sensed, were enjoying themselves, too. Throughout much of the match, there was a hush in the stadium, distinct from the febrile atmosphere of previous days. It wasn't the quietness of indifference but of heightened absorption, of 12,000 minds fixed on a single object. In some ways it resembled the quietness of an art gallery. For the most part, the match wasn't particularly tense. Nor was Federer playing exceptionally brilliantly. But there was a feeling, nonetheless, of something intricate revealing itself, the watching of which was riveting.

This can be put another way. When Federer plays, the tension often has less to do with the match itself—who is on top, what the score line is—than with the ebbs and flows of his own performance. On every point, there's a hope—even an expectation—that he'll do something magical. Accordingly, the sighs that greet his misses don't necessarily express disappointment at the point he's lost; more a sense of a vision not being fulfilled. The other player can seem almost irrelevant in all this; his role becomes little more than that of facilitator, pacemaker. Federer's habit of feeding catches to the ball boys—as if challenging them to keep up—reinforces the sense of divided attention. It's as if the match itself is not enough, but one element in a multilayered drama, just another level of the game.

At the very end, there was a sudden lurch in tone, focused intensity giving way to bathos. The second set went to a tiebreak, which Federer won with a point at the net. People leapt to their feet, began cheering; Nishikori walked to the net. But Federer turned and headed back to the baseline, as if readying himself for another point. For a second, doubt flicked through my mind. Was Federer playing some kind of trick? Could we all have got it wrong? But no: the winner of the match appeared to be in a daze, oblivious of the fact that he had won it. Eventually he looked up, realized his mistake and, now smiling, turned once more, and ran to the net.

3.

Afterwards, I headed out for another *Mett* sandwich. It seemed a good way—an apt way—to celebrate. After all, I'd eaten a *Mett* sandwich the last time Federer had won, and his next match had been victorious. Federer's chances of success were clearly tied to my consumption of raw pork. I didn't linger because Nishikori was about to do a "mixed session" outside the player's entrance—a sort of interview-to-camera-cum-standing press conference. When I arrived, a crowd was gathered behind some railings. Children were clutching those fluffy, oversized balls that players sign. The dancing bear from earlier was ambling about.

Nishikori came out, and a small gaggle of journalists—mostly Japanese—crowded round him. Up close, he looked even scrawnier than he had on court. There was nothing to him apart from bone and muscle. When my turn came, I asked how different Federer had seemed today from their last encounter, in Miami, which Nishikori had won. "He was much better, definitely," he said. "It wasn't the same as playing him on a hard court. He was so fast, serving well, volleying a lot. He really made me struggle."

Dinesh, the correspondent from Bangalore, was also there, and he leaned in towards Nishikori, trying to get his tape recorder as close as possible but looking, for an instant, as if he was going to hug him. Nishikori, demonstrating the flexibility and core strength that all top tennis players possess, simply stayed where he was and tilted his torso backwards, as if approaching a limbo bar. An ATP official a few feet away sprang forward and prized Dinesh away. "For fuck's sake, not so close to the player!" he commanded. The impediment cleared, Nishikori returned to upright and—unperturbed—carried on answering questions.

4.

I headed up to the press box cafeteria, which overlooked the court. Federer's doubles was already underway; his press conference would start as soon as it was over. I wanted some time to gather my thoughts, to ready myself. I'd managed to attend a Federer press conference once before, after his loss to Djokovic in the group stage of the 2013 World Tour Finals. On that occasion, the room had been crowded, and my eagerly raised hand had been ignored. But here, where there were hardly any other English-speaking journalists, it seemed likely that I'd get to ask a question—possibly several. It suddenly dawned on me that this might be the one opportunity I would ever have to converse directly, one-to-one, with Federer. What on earth should I ask?

My first thought was to think of something clever and technical, a question that would demonstrate to him how detailed my knowledge of tennis was, prove that I was something more than a run-of-the-mill hack. But then I thought: hang on. What I really wanted to ask was either something larger, or even narrower. I wanted to tell him that I was writing a book about him, and ask him how he felt about that. I wanted to ask what his feelings were about the widespread fascination, the obsession, he inspires. Did he understand it? Could he explain it? Did it unnerve him? I wanted to ask him about his forehand, how he came to play the shot in that particular way, and what goes through his mind when he does something particularly outrageous. I wanted to ask him about life chez Federer—what his relationship with Mirka was really like, how much time he spent with his children. But I knew that these types of questions would be impossible, off-limits. This was a press conference, not a tête-à-tête between old friends.

My ruminations were soon broken off by the appearance of Dinesh, who seemed unbothered by his recent skirmish with authority. We got talking, first about Federer, and then—for reasons I can't now precisely recall—about speed guns. Dinesh was most exercised by what he claimed was the problem of their inconsistent readings. Serves at the French Open, he said, were not as fast as serves at Wimbledon. Such discrepancies were inevitable given the way that speed guns worked, dividing the length of the court by the time it took for the ball to travel from one baseline to the other.

I was somewhat taken aback by this. Speed guns, I pointed out, surely measured the ball's speed at just a single point on its journey, presumably right after being hit. The calculation couldn't be based on the ball's progress down the whole length of the court, as that would mean that postbounce velocity would have to be taken into account, and since bounce is dependent on court speed, the readings would become meaningless. If, as he claimed, average speeds were slower at the French Open than at Wimbledon, then that was presumably because players' struck their serves less forcefully at Roland Garros, knowing that they couldn't get such an advantage from them. "But that is clearly wrong," Dinesh replied. "The only way to calculate speed is to divide distance by time. So there have to be two cameras, fixed at different points, which measure both the ball's distance and its time and then calculate the speed from that. This is basic physics."

It rapidly became clear that this was going to be a fundamental point of disagreement between us. I didn't see how Dinesh's "two-cameras" theory could work, even if the second gun was fixed not at the baseline but at the net (which he conceded it might be). The ball's differing angles and trajectories would mean that the distance it traveled would never be the same, rendering the readings meaningless. The technology *had* to be more sophisticated than that. Yet nothing I said could persuade Dinesh. He clung to his two-cameras position with astonishing tenacity, even claiming, at one point, that the fact that wide serves receive slower readings than down-the-middle ones *proved* him right, because wide serves had a greater distance to travel. (Actually, I pointed out, it's because wide serves *are* slower than down-the-middle ones, either because they have more spin or players strike them more gently so as to increase their chances of getting the ball in.)

The argument meandered on and on, becoming—at least on my side—increasingly bad-tempered. The problem was that I didn't know definitively how speed guns worked either (and Dinesh knew I didn't). All I could do was point out, *a priori*, that his theory was incorrect, based on the fact that it would make a mockery of the whole system. But this was the one thing that Dinesh seemed unbothered by. He thought it eminently possible that pundits and analysts had been citing inaccurate data for years, not aware that the system was fundamentally meaningless. There was a naïveté to this viewpoint that I found remarkable. I wanted to shake him out of his irrationality.

The argument never did get resolved—although I was relieved to discover subsequently, on checking, that I had been right. But what it did most efficiently was waste my precious preparation time. Suddenly, I looked down at the court and saw that the doubles was over. Federer and Chiudinelli had won in straight sets. A couple of minutes later, an announcement came on the tannoy: Federer's press conference was about to begin. I suddenly felt panicked and deeply annoyed. Instead of formulating my killer question, I'd wasted more than an hour on an entirely fatuous argument. My feelings towards Dinesh became even more aggressive. I'd messed up, and it was all his fault.

5.

On the way over to the conference room, I desperately tried to think of something to ask. By now I'd abandoned all notions of trying to look clever. I just wanted to sound vaguely plausible, not to come across as an idiot. There were twenty or so journalists in the room. Most were German. Federer walked in, wearing a tracksuit and cap. He sat down, gave us a quick smile, and then the official announced that there would be a few English-language questions before the German ones started. I raised my hand, along with two or three others (including Dinesh, who was sitting next to me), and was taken aback when the official pointed straight at me. I was first! So I went for it. "This week," I said, "we've seen a lot of serve and volley. Dustin Brown did it all the time. And today, in the second set, there were games when you came in behind every serve. Do you think it is possible that we could be seeing a return of serve and volley? And if so, would you regard that as a good thing?"

All things considered, I didn't think it was a bad question. I was surprised—and relieved—by how fluently it came out. Moreover, it appeared to go down well. There were titters around the room while I was speaking and then Federer himself—yes, Federer!—smiled. He smiled *at me*. He evidently thought that what I'd said was funny! "Yes, I think it would be a good thing because so few people today do it," he said. "And having a contrast between baseline and serve and volley is always nice." (At this point I interjected: "And of course, your heroes when you were growing up, Edberg and Sampras, served and volleyed." "Exactly," Federer replied. As you can see, we were becoming positively chummy.) "But I don't think just because of two days of tennis we are going to see the game changing entirely," Federer continued. "You can do it here to a certain extent, because the courts are a bit faster than at Wimbledon. There, where the guys have just a bit more time on their returns, it's not so easy."

Federer's answer was so equable and attentive that for a moment I forgot the reality of the situation. It really did feel like the two of us were having a private chat, which we could have carried on for hours. But then his words stopped, the official pointed to the next person, and I was brought back to my surroundings. In truth it hadn't been much, just a minute or so of eye contact, of dialogue. Yet for that time I'd had Federer all to myself, and it felt wonderful.

Halle, Sunday, June 15, 2014

1.

I began my final day in Halle by interviewing Dustin Brown. We spoke in the lobby of the Gerry Weber Sportpark Hotel (which meant I finally got to walk down Roger-Federer-Allee). Brown was talkative and intense, and managed to combine being lively and sharp with giving the impression of being fundamentally uninterested in all my questions. He told me about his early days on the Futures and Challenger circuits, when, as a cost-saving measure, he'd driven a camper van from tournament to tournament, using whatever prize money he earned at one event to buy his petrol to get to the next. He talked about the racism he had been subjected to as a child growing up in provincial Germany, and which he still sometimes encountered as an adult. It was exciting to have the chance to interview him, and I enjoyed writing up the piece. But I couldn't help but feel that I'd got the wrong man. As we talked, I kept half an eye out for Federer, but he didn't appear.

That afternoon, in the final, Federer played Alejandro Falla, the Columbian left-hander who'd taken him to five sets in the first round at Wimbledon in 2010. Despite Federer's difficulties then—when he'd been playing unusually poorly—there wasn't any doubt who would win today. The Nishikori match had felt like the real final. In fact, Falla played well, and managed to force tiebreaks in both sets. But Federer raised his game enough to win them convincingly. Afterwards, there was a prize-giving ceremony and speeches in German. It was Federer's seventh win at Halle.

During the half-hour gap before the doubles final started, Federer gave another press conference. And so I got a second bite at the cherry. Emboldened by my success the previous day, I thought I'd try and make Federer laugh again. "Roger," I said. "Congratulations on your victory today. But aren't you getting a bit bored of winning Halle all the time? When are you going to come to Queen's instead?"

This time, my question completely bombed. The room fell silent, and Federer looked utterly stony-faced. "You will never see me at Queen's," he said in a flat voice. "I have a lifetime contract to play at Halle. So long as the two tournaments are played at the same time, I will always be at Halle, not London." He added that he had played at Queen's early in his career, and had lost in the first round. "So my experience there was not very happy."

I felt crushed, foolish. I should, of course, have known about his lifetime contract, but after the last press conference, I'd imagined that Federer would somehow be well disposed towards me, that he would immediately get the jokiness of my question, laugh along with me. And wouldn't he be in a lighthearted mood, having just won the tournament? But instead my question appeared to irritate him. Did he consider it disrespectful? Or was it so idiotic that he simply didn't think it was worth bothering to engage properly with? Whatever the case, my high spirits abruptly departed. I had gone from making Federer laugh to earning his displeasure. It wasn't a nice feeling.

2.

I watched the doubles final (another thrilling match, which Federer and Chiudinelli ended up losing on a championship tiebreak), but my thoughts were already drifting homewards. Afterwards, I had a valedictory *Mett* sandwich, but this time it didn't taste quite so good. As I was eating it, it occurred to me that putting so much raw pork inside myself was actually quite disgusting. It was my fourth *Mett* sandwich in as many days. I suddenly saw myself through my wife's eyes. (She is a vegetarian.) It was definitely time to get back to England.

Dinesh was on the station platform at Halle—he was going back to his hotel in a nearby town called Bielefeld. We got talking to another of the Backpack Babes, a Brazilian woman in her sixties called Marcia who had short, purple-rinsed hair, a battered face, sad eyes. She had traveled all the way from Rio to see Federer. She'd been at the French Open, and had a Centre Court ticket during the first week at Wimbledon. She was desperately hoping that Federer would be playing that day. ("But if he isn't I'll find another way.") She told us that she could only afford tickets for the first week; the second was too expensive. She said that she'd fallen in love with tennis in 1975, when she'd watched Arthur Ashe beat Jimmy Connors in the Wimbledon final. She'd later loved Edberg and Sampras, but after that had stopped being so interested. Then she'd seen Federer for the first time in 2008. "As soon as I saw him, I said to myself, 'This man is not playing tennis. He is creating art.'" This meant, I said, that she'd missed his great years. "Yes," she said ruefully. "I didn't have Roger for all that time. I missed him." She could have been describing a lover.

Dinesh mentioned Nadal and Marcia's eyes instantly narrowed. "How I hate that man. How I loathe him. He is not a nice person. He is a cheat. Always talking about his injuries. Always using the time out. But it's not just that. It's also his game. He only does one thing. He has no variety."

I would have liked to have carried on talking to Marcia. There was a soulfulness to her that was both attractive and intriguing. It struck me that she embodied a certain type of fanship—a deeply romantic, passionate type whose inspiration was more artistic than anything else. But her stop soon came, and she had to get out. "Perhaps I'll see you at Wimbledon," she said. Dinesh and I carried on to Bielefeld together. We didn't return to the subject of speed guns.

chapter six

The pursuit of beauty

1.

That Roger Federer plays exceptionally attractive tennis is a truth that is widely—if not universally—acknowledged. But opinions differ as to what to make of this fact.

One approach is to respond with a shrug. Federer's tennis may be aesthetically pleasing—but so what? Sport is about winning, not looking pretty. Character matters because it directly bears on success. A strong-minded athlete will be more likely to hold his nerve when things get tough; a weak-minded one won't. But qualities like grace, elegance, effortlessness, and litheness are mere superfluities, distractions from what really counts. A backhand that's pleasing to the eye won't necessarily win the point.

Linked to this attitude of broad indifference is another, more avowedly hostile approach. This line of thinking holds that beauty is a kind of betrayal of what sport is about. Sport, according to this view, is a rugged, macho enterprise that is practical and goal-orientated. To suggest that aesthetics have a role to play is to vitiate its masculine steadfastness. It is to introduce a feminine concern with ornamentation into a sphere in which such considerations don't belong. This view takes the apparent uselessness of beauty in sport—the fact that a purpose can't easily be assigned to it—as a sign of its inherent worthlessness. To attach importance to something that doesn't have a clear role is to get one's priorities all jumbled up.

A player like Federer, therefore, could be seen as a challenge to the hearty, goal-orientated, phallocentric view of sport—the view that, I would suggest, currently predominates in our sporting culture, and which, to a large extent, always has. For this reason, it is unsurprising that criticisms of Federer so often center on his masculinity. Mats Wilander said that he lacked balls, but that is just one example of a strain of Federer-related opprobrium that seeks to suggest that there is something insufficiently rugged about the seventeen-times Grand Slam champion, that despite his success (and the fact, let's not forget, that he has four children) he isn't a "real" man. Such abuse, it goes without saying, is especially rampant in Nadal-supporting online forums, where Federer is routinely described in highly emasculating (and even, strangely, homophobic) terms. But it must also be conceded that Federer has, at various stages of his career, done a certain amount to encourage this attitude himself, chiefly by dressing up in silly costumes and willingly turning himself into a fashion icon.[1] In a way, though, that Federer so easily acceded to this public dandification is merely a testament to the irresistibility of the symbolism, to the insidious nature of the pressures that exist. If a male tennis player is attractive to watch, he must, almost by definition, be excessively fey and image-conscious.[2]

A third response to Federer's attractiveness is to treat it positively. Yes, Federer plays singularly beautiful tennis, and yes, this is important. Whether or not it has anything to do with how often he wins, it's one of the things (actually, *the* thing) that makes him so appealing, so special. It should be openly acknowledged and celebrated. This, naturally, is my view—and, I'm sure, that of most of his fans. But it leads to a difficult question. What exactly *is* it about Federer's play that makes it so aesthetically pleasing? What does it mean for an athlete to be beautiful?

---

1. He recently admitted that he now regrets some of his more flamboyant outfits, such as, presumably, the white-and-gold-embossed military outfit he wore at Wimbledon in 2009.

2. Elizabeth Wilson points out that, in the first half of the twentieth century, male tennis players were routinely labeled "sissies." Merely to play such an effete game, if you were a man, was to lay yourself open to having your sexuality called into question.

2.

Sport has never been all that comfortable with beauty. Although it is widely acknowledged that certain athletes—Muhammad Ali, Nadia Comaneci, David Gower, Michael Jordan—have been exceptionally graceful, sport as a whole doesn't have much of a tradition of talking about the subject. The tendency, both of writers and fans, has been to pay beauty a sort of grudging lip service—to acknowledge it when it occurs, and move swiftly on. Football, of course, is known as the "beautiful game," but that doesn't mean that its beauty is really talked about, much less properly analyzed. This isn't the case in other fields. The history of art is littered with books about beauty and aesthetics. People have always waxed lyrical about—and tried to analyze—the beauty of nature. The attractiveness (or otherwise) of people's bodies and faces is likewise endlessly discussed. Even mathematicians talk about "beautiful proofs." But sport, despite being an immensely popular and well-chronicled pursuit, singularly lacks a discourse of this kind.

This failure to engage with beauty in any depth has a number of causes—some fairly obvious, some a bit less so. First, there's the fact that describing, let alone analyzing, beauty is inherently difficult. Beauty is a nebulous concept at the best of times; there's a sense in which it lies beyond words. What is it? Is it a property of an object (a rose, a sunset) or is it, as the saying goes, in the eye of the beholder? Does it have some kind of connection to morality, to goodness, or are its attractions of a purely formal nature? In light of such complexities, it isn't entirely surprising that, when analyzing sport, people generally ignore beauty and concentrate on more tangible things. Why dissect the gracefulness of Federer's serve when you could instead focus on how often he gets his first delivery in, what its speed is, or where he hits it in the box?

Secondly, and no doubt connected to this, there's the urge many people have, upon encountering beauty, to fall silent, as if to say anything at all would be disrespectful. There's a sense that beauty inspires wordlessness not just because of its complexity, but because there's a certain "correct" attitude to adopt when confronted by it—one of mute contemplation. This connects to the idea, which originated in the late eighteenth century, that what defines beauty, above all, is the attitude people take to it. There is such a thing as an "aesthetic gaze"—a state of mind a person has to be in in order to be receptive to beauty.

Thirdly, as I've already hinted, there's also the fact that sport (or, at any rate, sporting culture) has traditionally been a masculine domain, in which male values are to the fore. And men, at least in today's world, aren't always comfortable thinking and talking about beauty. There is, in fact, a curious contradiction, or double standard, in the male sporting attitude. On the one hand, there's a clear homoerotic undertow to much of what goes on: a fascination with physical display, the prowess of the male body, the licensed tactility of the goal celebration. And yet there's a strange silence surrounding such matters, as if to talk about them at all would leave men exposed to the risk of having their masculinity questioned.[3]

In addition, there are a couple of less obvious explanations for sport's reticence on this subject—one historical, the other theoretical. Sport only developed a strong culture of its own in the first half of the twentieth century; the 1920s and 1930s were when watching sport became a really popular pastime, when the concept of "the fan" originated, and when sports writing got going. And it was around this period that our attitude towards beauty fundamentally changed. In art and literature, Modernism was on the rise; it prized discordance and difficulty. Beauty not only became less central to the project of art than it had been in previous centuries; art was explicitly turned against it. As the Abstract Impressionist painter Barnett Newton baldly put it: the impulse of modern art was to "destroy beauty." Nor were philosophers offering much help; they had already largely abandoned their own centuries-long quest to define beauty, having conceded that, since it was impossible to establish it as anything other than subjective, they were basically banging their heads against the wall. In addition, beauty increasingly fell victim to various

---

3. I don't mean to imply here that women's relationship with beauty is, by contrast, straightforward. It isn't. And one reason for this is sexism—which exists to a quite worrying extent in sport. Women athletes are routinely denigrated either for not being feminine enough or, when they do embrace their femininity, for being provocative. Both sets of charges have been leveled at women tennis players throughout the history of the sport. Nonetheless, I do think that men have a tendency to be particularly tight-lipped on the subject of beauty, and that this is one of the reasons why sporting aesthetics haven't been properly grappled with.

political critiques, which linked it to unjustifiable privilege and social oppression.

The confluence of these trends has led some to suggest that, in the first half of the twentieth century, at least in the West, a "flight from beauty" occurred.[4] Humanity collectively turned its back on a concept that had been central to its outlook and identity for millennia. Given this, is it really so surprising that sport—an activity, after all, that only acquired mass appeal during the twentieth century—has never had a great deal to say about it?

The theoretical reason for sport's lack of engagement with beauty is related to the question—already touched on—of what sport is really about. In his essay on Federer, David Foster Wallace wrote that "Beauty is not the goal of competitive sports, but high-level sports are a prime venue for the expression of human beauty. The relationship is roughly that of courage to war." The key point here is that beauty isn't inherent to sport's ends. Athletes don't set out to be beautiful; they set out to win, just as soldiers, to extend Wallace's analogy, don't set out to be courageous; they set out to vanquish the enemy.[5] Whatever beauty results from sport is in the nature of a by-product. It may be praiseworthy, but it isn't essential.

Art is of course different. When beauty is present in, say, a

---

4. This is the phrase the philosopher Roger Scruton uses in his short, useful book on the subject, *Beauty*.

5. Actually, I'm not sure that Wallace's analogy holds: while courage isn't the point of war, it does have a function—to make soldiers fight more fiercely. In other words, it isn't entirely incidental to war's aims, in the way that beauty arguably is to sport's.

Mozart string quartet, or a Titian painting, it is there, we can feel confident, because the artist specifically intended it to be. Beauty is inherent to art's objectives, and is therefore something that those who consume art expect—even demand—to encounter. This point holds even after the beauty-rejecting influence of Modernism is taken into account. When art is not beautiful—even when it is explicitly ugly—that fact is still likely to be seen as a statement of some kind. The artist's attitude to beauty—whether embracing or rejecting—remains integral to the work's objectives. Beauty and ugliness, in art, are never just by-products.

Wallace's suggestion that beauty isn't the "goal" of competitive sports doesn't hold true in every case, of course. There are sports—gymnastics, diving—in which points are awarded for aesthetic merit. In such cases, beauty stops being a by-product and becomes incorporated into the sport's competitive aims. The more graceful a gymnast, the more likely she is to win. (This itself raises thorny theoretical issues to do with whether beauty should ever be put to such nakedly instrumental use.) It's fair to say, however, that in the large majority of sports, including tennis, there is no necessary link between being attractive and being victorious.

3.

One of the oldest ideas about beauty is that it stems from a sense of order and proportion. This was the conception of beauty that was most prevalent in the classical world. It is expressed, for example, by Aristotle in the *Poetics,* when he writes that, "to be beautiful, a living creature, and every whole made up of parts, must . . . present a certain order in its arrangement of parts." This conception of beauty is fundamentally relational: beauty consists in an object having "parts" that fit well together. The most straightforward manifestation of the idea is symmetry. Symmetrical objects are beautiful because their elements look similar to one another. Reflection is inherently pleasing.

Of course, this conception of beauty isn't confined to objects that are symmetrical—that would be rather limiting. The idea has a looser application in the principles of harmony and balance. Harmony is somewhat similar to symmetry, but implies broad resemblance rather than near-exact concordance. For instance, a motif that recurs in various forms throughout a piece of music might be said to contribute to its overall harmoniousness. Balance, unlike harmony, implies contrast. A painting featuring a dark, hemmed-in foreground and a light, open background might well be described as balanced; likewise a play that features both tragedy and comedy. Aesthetically, in other words, balance can be seen as a way of making opposing elements complement one another.

These ideas have had a huge impact on the way beauty has been understood over the centuries. They were highly influential during the Renaissance, when artists such as Piero della Francesca and Leonardo da Vinci based the composition of their paintings on mathematical formulas—such as the "Golden Ratio"—that were thought to embody principles of harmony and proportion. They were integral to the neoclassicism of the eighteenth century. And, despite last century's supposed "flight from beauty," they continue to bear on what we consider attractive today. The Taj Mahal is considered one of the world's most iconic buildings because it so clearly embodies the principles of symmetry and harmony. Faces (and bodies) that are in proportion are generally thought to be more appealing. To describe a work of art as "unbalanced" would be to seriously impugn its aesthetic merits.

This conception of beauty is relevant to Federer, too. Virtually everything about the Swiss seems balanced, in proportion. His body has no Nadalesque asymmetries. His tennis is frequently described as "complete." He is equally happy at the net or baseline. He can defend brilliantly as well as attack, and switch very quickly between the two. He uses an equivalent grip (modified Eastern) on both wings and even his backhand and forehand volleys look strangely alike, sharing the same distinctive high back lift. He is literally balanced, too, in the sense that he falls over less than other players.[6] And the concept applies, more generally, to his personality—to the way, for instance, he combines playing professional tennis with being a husband and father and how he never seems stressed or pushed for time.

This particular theory of beauty wasn't the only one that existed in the ancient world. There was also the Platonic, or idealist, conception. The key concept here wasn't proportion but *unity*. At the heart of Plato's philosophy is the idea of a hierarchy

---

6. This was illustrated most gratifyingly at Wimbledon in 2014, when, towards the end of the tournament, the grass behind the Centre Court baselines became exceedingly worn. When Dimitrov and Djokovic played their semifinal, both players slipped all over the place. Then Federer came out for his match against Raonic, and didn't stumble once.

of forms that binds everything in the universe together. Every object in the material sphere has a prototype in the world of ideals. A cup can be the object I drink my coffee out of or an abstract entity that represents the ideal form of cupness. The more my cup resembles this ideal, the better (and also, very probably, the more beautiful) it will be. (Ultimate values such as goodness, truth and beauty are, in Plato's scheme, closely related.) Like all things, beauty itself partakes of the hierarchy; it can manifest itself at higher and lower levels. Plato illustrated this, most famously, with the idea (to modern eyes an exceedingly strange one) of a "ladder of beauty" that starts with the sexual desire an older man feels for a boy and progresses up through various stages of beauty-appreciation until pederastic desire is finally transmuted into the love of absolute beauty itself.

In idealist philosophy, the concept of beauty is closely linked to that of perfection. Objects become more beautiful the more ideal—the more perfect—they are. Beauty points upwards, provides a link between the material and divine spheres. This idea of beauty, too, has profoundly influenced our culture. During the Middle Ages, it found various expressions in Christian theology, including in the idea that material objects—such as Gothic cathedrals—offered windows on to the heavenly realms. It was central to the German Idealist movement of the nineteenth century, influencing thinkers such as Hegel and Schiller. And it lies at the root of the persistent attempts—which continue today in the work of philosophers such as Martha Nussbaum and Elaine Scarry—to forge a connection between beauty and morality.

Once again, this conception of beauty is pertinent to Federer. After all, his tennis is often described as perfect (or, as his more ardent fans like to put it, "peRFect"). When people say this, they don't simply mean that his game is flawless. The sentiment is more active: they are imputing a moral quality to his tennis, suggesting that he somehow plays the game as it *should* be played. What is perfect, after all, must also be right. This helps make sense of the overblown, frankly disproportionate pain committed fans such as myself so often experience when Federer loses. Our trauma is not mainly, or only, caused by the fact that we feel sorry for him; it is more to do with our sense that some fundamental wrong, some injustice, has been perpetrated. The *New Yorker* writer Nick Paumgarten accurately captured this feeling in a piece he wrote following Federer's semifinal defeat by Djokovic at the 2011 US Open. "The point is that to root for Federer is to root for a Platonic ideal," Paumgarten wrote. "It is like rooting for the truth."[7]

These conceptions of beauty go a long way to explaining the visual appeal of Federer's tennis. His game taps into ideas about beauty, inherited from the ancient world, that are deeply ingrained within our culture. But is there anything more to add? Are there dimensions to Federer's tennis that these theories miss? During the early years of my obsession, I would probably have said no. I accepted the idea that Federer was—as the American essayist Joseph Epstein has put it—"a pure type of the Apollonian."[8] But nowadays, I'm not so sure. Increasingly, I have come to believe that what Federer

---

7. "Big Shot," *New Yorker*, September 11, 2011.

8. "How Roger Federer Lost His Topspin," *Newsweek*, April 17, 2009.

appears to be on the surface—all classical orderliness, clean perfection—is deceptive. The standard picture we have of him isn't wholly accurate. If you look closer—into, as it were, the marrow of his game—he starts to seem less ordered and neat, more jagged and even a bit chaotic. Two things have led me to this conclusion. One is my realization that Federer's technique and strategy are more complicated than they first appear, that they are at least as much about discordance and disruption as about order and harmony (especially, as I've suggested, on his forehand). The other thing that has caused me to think this is the experience of watching him live—and, especially, from really close up.

4.

In the summer of 2010, my girlfriend discovered she was pregnant. It wasn't planned, but the news was good. We were in our midthirties. We both knew—although we perhaps hadn't fully admitted it yet—that we were going to stay together. All seemed well until we went for the twelve-week scan. The radiologist who saw us didn't seem very clued up, and although he didn't say anything specific, something in his manner—a certain offhand vagueness—made us feel uneasy. So we arranged to see a different doctor, a specialist in fetal medicine. Within a few minutes of embarking upon his scan, he told us—with the bluntness of genuine expertise—that something was seriously wrong. The baby's organs didn't appear to be developing properly. He couldn't see any kidneys.

The specialist's immediate suspicion was that the problem was a rare chromosomal abnormality, a bit like Down syndrome but much more serious. He performed something called a CVS—which involved taking a cell sample from the placenta—and told us that we would have the results in a week. The results came back negative: there was no chromosomal disorder, but he was still convinced that something was very wrong. Over the next few weeks, the doctor performed further scans. These confirmed that the development was indeed abnormal. Instead of kidneys, the baby had a collection of cysts. This affected the amniotic fluid and meant, in turn, that its lungs couldn't develop. It could make it to full term, but it wouldn't survive after birth. We therefore had two options: either my girlfriend could carry the baby to term and give birth, knowing that it would certainly die. Or we could have a termination. The latter seemed like our only real choice, but in order for the doctors to get a clearer picture of exactly what the problem was, my girlfriend was advised that she should wait until eighteen weeks to have the termination. For six weeks, she had to carry a fetus that she knew was unviable. And in the end, the diagnosis was still inconclusive. The baby had an extremely rare type of cloacal disorder, the causes of which were unknown.

The termination took place on a Tuesday. It was, unsurprisingly, a miserable time—a brutal negation of the future, of our hopes. We were both devastated, but we dealt with it very differently. My girlfriend, understandably griefstricken, wanted closeness, intimacy. But I ran away from my feelings—and, by extension, from her. As ever, I sought refuge in tennis. This was the week of the World Tour Finals. Federer won his three group matches, all in straight sets. I managed to get to one of them, an afternoon match against Robin Söderling, slipping out from work at lunchtime and riding my scooter down to the Greenwich peninsula, a journey I've undertaken several times over the years. Federer played well enough—he won 6–4, 7–6. I also managed to get to a couple of the group stage evening sessions, when Federer wasn't playing. In fact I spent most of that week either at work or at the O2. Looking back, I can see how odd, and how selfish, my behavior was. My girlfriend was left feeling hurt and abandoned.

Federer's semifinal—against Djokovic—was on Saturday night. That weekend, my girlfriend and I were intending to take things easy, but on Saturday afternoon I suggested that we at least look into the possibility of getting tickets. Watching tennis, I said, might be a useful way to take our minds off what had happened. Rather remarkably, she agreed: I think by this point she despairingly felt that if she couldn't beat me, she might as well join me. Luck, too, conspired to assist us. On eBay, I found an ad for a pair of front section seats. I spoke to the seller on the phone. He and his wife were Murray fans, down from Glasgow. That afternoon they'd seen Murray lose a long, thrilling match to Nadal. Rather than watching more tennis, they fancied a consoling evening in the pub. I can remember the sense of urgency that descended upon us and that summoned us from our dolorous state. The match was due to start in little more than an hour. We drove to the O2 through the early evening traffic, met our Caledonian benefactors outside the Slug and Lettuce, traded cash for tickets. And then, miraculously, there we were in the arena, in the *second row*, level with the baseline; seats much better than anything I'd hoped for.

Though by this point I'd seen Federer live quite a few times, I'd never been this close to him before. And here's the thing: it makes a massive difference. When you're that close, you begin to understand something that isn't normally quite graspable, which is that the person before you isn't the familiar, two-dimensional TV icon but a flesh-and-blood being, no different from anyone else, sweating, breathing, with creases in his shorts. As if for the first time, you realize that what he is attempting to do—controlling a small object being smashed towards him at breakneck speed—is mind-bogglingly difficult, terrifying in a way, something entirely outside the realm of normal human accomplishment. In theory, of course, I already knew these things. But actually seeing them so close up made me *really* know them. Distance lends an air of predictability, of safety, to tennis. Only when you're courtside do you understand its true precariousness.

The character of Federer's game also changes. The gliding, the silkiness: they're less obvious. You realize that, to a large extent, they're illusions—a product of scale, of watching speed from distance. Up close, the dominant impression is of mesmerizing pace. The movement is constant, unbroken, relentless; there are no pauses for recovery, no split-second hesitations. There is something ferocious, almost feral, about it. From 5 or 7 yards away, Federer looks a lot less nice than he normally does.

It helped, of course, that he was playing so well. From the start he was all over Djokovic, bearing down on him, dismembering his game. He won the first set 6–1. At the start of the second set, his form dipped slightly, and Djokovic took a 3–0 lead. But Federer's brilliance soon returned and he overtook Djokovic, winning the set 6–4. Sitting immediately behind us was a young man, also with his girlfriend. He was chatty, a lecturing type, and before the match he outlined, for her benefit, all the things he liked about Federer. But once it got going, his talkativeness stopped. Instead he just repeated a single word over and over: "Genius."

I particularly remember one shot from that evening, a forehand stop volley late in the second set. Had I seen it on TV, I probably wouldn't have thought twice about it. Federer routinely pulls off strokes that, on the face of it, are more impressive. But because of where we were sitting, I could see that, actually, it was astounding, a small miracle. Djokovic hit his forehand passing shot phenomenally hard. He absolutely belted the ball. Yet not only did Federer move to his right and meet the ball in the precise center of his racket; he stripped it of virtually all its pace, leaving the exact amount necessary for it to drift over the net with all the airborne weightlessness of a dandelion clock. The contrast between before and after—between the savage incoming pace and the extreme outgoing delicacy—was remarkable. Such dramatic deceleration, apart from anything else, seemed to contravene the first law of thermodynamics (the one about energy never being created or destroyed but merely changing). What had Federer done with all that power?

5.

Seeing him that night clarified something for me. When you watch tennis on TV, or from back in the crowd, a kind of double minimization takes place. Not only does the court seem smaller and easier to navigate than it is; the game itself appears less difficult. It becomes tempting to fall into the trap of thinking that what you are watching, while impressive, isn't in fact so *very* outstanding, that what the players are doing isn't entirely removed from what you—on a good day, with the right amount of practice—would be capable of. This line of thinking, I suspect, is especially tempting if you yourself play the sport to a half-decent standard. In that case, it's hard to resist the urge to make comparisons, to insert yourself imaginatively into the scene before you. Look, you think, they're not serving *that* much faster than I can! Those are the kinds of mistakes I often make! I sometimes play shots as good as that! Distance, by making professional tennis seem less remote, more normal, creates a space for the ego to flourish.

But watch from up close, and such illusions are shattered. The true size of the gulf becomes starkly—cruelly—apparent. Take Federer's stop volley. I sometimes play stop volleys and, had I seen the shot on TV, I might well have begun mentally replaying various ones I've hit over the years, bolstering myself with the thought that mine weren't so dissimilar. Yet that night the absurdity of such an idea became clear. It was obvious that I could *never* play a shot like that, a shot, remember, that was more or less routine for Federer. If the ball was hit towards me with such force, I would be lucky to get my racket to it, let alone get it into court, let alone to a part of the court where Djokovic, one of the fastest people in the world round a tennis court, couldn't reach it.

What was strange about this realization was that it wasn't at all crushing. On the contrary, it was uplifting. Although it forced me to accept how trifling my abilities are, it was a genuine piece of knowledge, of truth—and as such it was welcome, instructive. My ego may have been cut down, but something more valuable arose in its place. I felt a sense of gratitude, of joyousness, merely to have witnessed such skill, to know that it was possible.[9]

The realization was helpful in another sense. Before our trip to the O2, things with my girlfriend had not been good. The events of the previous few weeks had driven us apart. I'd coped with it all in the worst possible way. But now a reconnection took place. I'd been using tennis as a means of escape—but that night it effected a kind of return. The beauty of Federer's play shook me from the confines of my ego and enabled me, once more, to see the true relations of the world. Denial gave way to lucidity; what had been distorted became clear. I was returned to myself, to my life, to my girlfriend,

---

9. The novelist J. M. Coetzee makes an observation similar to this, also regarding Federer, in *Here and Now,* a collection of his correspondence with Paul Auster. He recalls watching Federer play a crosscourt backhand volley, and describes the progression of his feelings: "One starts by envying Federer, one moves from there to admiring him, and one ends up neither envying nor admiring him but exalted at the revelation of what a human being—a being like oneself—can do." Coetzee describes this reaction as being similar to his response to "masterworks of art on which I have spent a lot of time."

WILLIAM SKIDELSKY

and it now seemed possible to properly confront what had happened, and to move on, together, into the future.

6.

Since that evening, since seeing Federer up close for the first time, I've thought slightly differently about his beauty. It's not so much that my previous image of him was shattered; more that it was added to, complicated. I realized that, beneath the smooth polished surface of his tennis, there's a kind of submerged savagery, a visceral quality that normally remains concealed. It's there, I think, at the level of rally construction, in the way that he constantly runs round his backhand and looks to create sharp probing off-angles, sending the ball to unfamiliar regions of the court, breaking down his opponents' structures. It's there in the deceptiveness of his technique, the way that he simultaneously appears classic and modern. And it's there in the nastiness that sometimes bubbles to the surface, the ugly rage that you feel lurks within him—that of the petulant, thirteen-year-old racket thrower who, in some part of himself, Federer must still be.

All this, it seems to me, makes Federer less the archetypal Apollonian hero and turns him into a more ambivalent figure. But what exactly? The Romantics had a particular way of thinking about beauty, as embodying both order and disorder. In his Preface to the *Lyrical Ballads*, for example, Wordsworth wrote of the "pleasure which the mind derives from the perception of similitude in dissimilitude." He was

214

suggesting that there could be an aesthetic value, for the poet, in employing the conventions of poetic meter while simultaneously diverging from them—in creating a poetry at once familiar and unknown. It seems to me the idea fits neatly with Federer's tennis, which, like much Romantic poetry, rests on its combination of the obviously conventional and the subtly unorthodox. In the eighteenth century, various thinkers also drew a distinction between the beautiful and the sublime. In general, while beauty was seen as being linked to order and reason, the sublime was associated with objects—particularly in nature—that were overwhelming, awe-inspiring: Alpine mountain ranges, dramatic storms. Kant said that whereas beauty was derived from "the form of the object having boundaries," the characteristic of the sublime was a sense of "boundlessness." Beauty typically inspired comfort, pleasure; the sublime engendered feelings of awe and terror (though these could also be pleasurable in their own way). The concept represented an expansion of the category of the aesthetic to include things that were less beautiful than ugly—although this was a special kind of ugliness that had its own magnificence. I think sublime is a good way to describe the more visceral aspects of Federer's tennis, although, at the same time, much about his game is straightforwardly beautiful, too. It is somehow typical of Federer that he manages to straddle the two concepts. His game is both comforting *and* terrifying; it is neat ordered gardens and vertiginous Alpine mountain ranges; both (one could say) Mozart and Metallica.

Wimbledon,
Thursday, June 26–
Wednesday, July 2, 2014

1.

I managed to continue my Federer binge at Wimbledon, picking up, as it were, from where I left off in Halle. I saw him three times on his passage to the final: in the second round, the last sixteen, and the quarterfinals. Ticketless at the start of the tournament, I tried every seat-obtaining method that I could think of. I grabbed a pair at the last minute online;[10]

---

10. It isn't widely known that it's possible to purchase Wimbledon tickets online. Every morning at 9 a.m., the All-England Club releases, via Ticketmas-

I camped; and I leaned heavily on friends and acquaintances, one of whom, miraculously, came good with a pair (no less!) of Centre Court debentures.

In the second round, on Centre Court, I watched Federer play Gilles Müller, a big-serving Luxembourgian left-hander. I went with my mother; our seats were near the back, behind the server's arm. Federer won quickly, almost casually, sending down a plethora of aces. Earlier that afternoon, we saw Nadal effortfully dispose of Lukas Rosol, his conqueror in the second round two years earlier. Rosol, playing brilliantly, won the first set and had a point for a two-set lead, which he failed to take. Pettily, but amusingly, he exacted revenge by knocking over one of Nadal's meticulously placed water bottles while walking past at the change of ends. Nadal won the match in four sets.

Afterwards, I ran into Marcia—the Brazilian woman from the train in Halle. She'd been lucky: the one ticket she'd obtained for the championships had allowed her to see Federer. She told me that she was now heading to Paris, to stay with friends, but if Federer reached the final she'd try to come back.

For the fourth round, I camped. To buy turnstile tickets at Wimbledon, you have to join the queue; to be near enough its front to guarantee getting a pick of courts (which is to say,

---

ter, five hundred tickets for the next day's play on Centre, No. 1, and No. 2 Courts. Accordingly, every other weekday morning found me at my desk at 8:50 a.m., with PC, laptop, and iPad at the ready, poised to simultaneously apply for tickets on all three devices. This strategy had never borne fruit before, but this time it did.

in the first five hundred), you have to camp. I hate camping. In fact, it's something I'd managed to avoid completely for the best part of two decades. But fans have to be prepared to make big sacrifices, to step outside—in this case quite literally—their comfort zones. My one consolation was that there was no one else with me. There's only one thing worse than camping, and that's camping with other people.

Because of my dislike of camping, I possessed no kit. So on Sunday afternoon I visited Decathlon, the sports equipment store, and purchased a very reasonably priced one-man tent and a sleeping bag. I was relieved to discover that equipment had moved on since when I'd last camped, and that manufacturers were now giving at least some thought to comfort. Particularly welcome was the option to buy an inflatable mattress, rather than one of the thin roll-up mats that had once been ubiquitous (and which always seemed to result in a spectacularly achy body). The mattress necessitated a portable foot pump, and I threw in an inflatable pillow for good measure, but stopped short—after consulting my wife—at a first-aid kit and a full set of waterproofs.

Anxious not to take any chances, I turned up at Wimbledon at nine a.m. on Monday morning; Federer was due to play his fourth round match against Tommy Robredo on Tuesday afternoon.[11] The queue begins in a field about a mile up the road from the All England Club. I was given a

_____

11. Because of rain delays during the first week, the second-week schedule was rearranged, which is why some fourth round matches were being played on the Tuesday, not on Monday as usual.

ticket that identified me as eighty-second in line—in other words, I could have arrived much later. No sooner did I take my place than a red-faced man in his seventies—one of Wimbledon's volunteer army of stewards—instructed me to erect my tent, although he added that I shouldn't yet peg it in. I managed to accomplish this without too much difficulty, but I encountered problems when it came to using my foot pump to inflate my mattress. The steward, who was keeping a watchful eye on things, came over and snappily said: "Young man, I think you'll find that you've attached the tube to the deflate outlet." He then proceeded to apply his brogue-clad foot to the pump with a vigor that struck me as unmistakably military.

The queue was steadily growing around me; everywhere there were people busying themselves with rucksacks and sleeping bags and an assortment of canvas paraphernalia. There was a general air of industriousness, of collective preparation; although what we were preparing ourselves for was to remain in the exact same position for the best part of twenty-four hours. The English people in my section of the queue were mainly in their teens or late twenties and, to judge by their accents, expensively educated. There was also a substantial foreign contingent, including a quartet of young Korean women just in front of me and, a couple of spaces back, a Taiwanese family of three, who had one of the most sophisticated-looking tents I've ever seen—they appeared to erect it by pressing a button. Immediately behind me, in stark contrast, was an insouciant seventeen-year-old who was also camping solo but who, unlike me, had arrived with only a sleeping bag. When the stewards asked him about this, he mumbled: "Um, yeah, well, my friend was going to come, and he was bringing the tent, but he dropped out, so I just thought I'd come anyway." This triggered grave concern among the stewards, who seemed to doubt whether it was medically possible to survive the rigors of an English summer night in the open. Eventually, one of them traipsed off and returned with a tent that a previous camper had left behind.

This, my neighbor now set about trying to erect. But he appeared to lack even a rudimentary knowledge of the principles of tent construction, because he got the outer and inner linings mixed up. Flush from my own recent success, I offered to help, but it soon became evident that there was either something wrong with the tent, or it was designed in some highly irregular way, because no matter what we did, we just couldn't make the thing stand up. After a while, the father of the Taiwanese family, observing our travails, came over and, with a certain formality, offered his assistance. The three of us worked together on the recalcitrant tent and eventually, after much head-scratching and tangling of guy ropes, managed to wrestle it into a habitable condition, although it was still somewhat lopsided. "No wonder it was fucking abandoned," was my neighbor's verdict when we'd finished.

Once all our tents were up, the stewards ordered a kind of mass compression; we were instructed to move down the line as far as possible, so that the sides of our tents were jammed up against the ones immediately in front of us. Only at this point were we allowed to peg them in. Soon another adjacent line formed (the queue crossed from one side of the field to the other and kept snaking back on itself), and its members were in turn required not merely to press themselves together as we had, but also to jam the backs of their tents directly onto ours. This approach no doubt made sense from a space-saving point of view, but it did mean that, save for the thinnest of partitions, we were all basically going to sleep with one another.

The rest of the day unfolded in a state of torpor. There was nothing to do, and we were told that we had to stay where we were, because at some unspecified point in the afternoon the all-important "blue dockets" would be handed out, which we'd need the following morning to obtain the wristbands that would, in turn, give us the right to buy our tickets. So, if we did anything untoward—like wander off to the pub—we would almost certainly lose our place. Therefore, I lounged on my mattress and read the book I'd brought with me, John McPhee's *Levels of the Game*. A classic of American sports journalism, it's an in-depth account of the 1968 US Open semifinal between Arthur Ashe and Clark Graebner. Both players were American, and both were serve and volleyers, but apart from that they couldn't have been more different: one was black, one was white; one was Democrat, the other (Graebner) was a staunch Republican; one (Ashe) played what the other regarded as a loose-wristed, liberal style, while the other's strokes were stiff and conservative. McPhee intersperses his account of the match with detailed portraits of the two players' backgrounds and their contrasting worldviews. Yet despite their differences, they had enormous respect for each other, and one of the book's strengths is the way it captures their affection.

It was a gripping read, but also a quick one. It took about two hours to finish the whole thing. Now I really had nothing to do, as I'd failed to bring any other reading matter. The only option was to have a nap.

2.

Sleep that night inevitably proved fitful. The stewards came round at about 10 p.m. and ordered "lights out," but cramming several teenagers into a small space has never been a recipe for easeful slumber and, thanks to the dense arrangements of the tents, there seemed to be several such groups within roughly three feet of where I was lying. There was nothing that I couldn't hear. A trio of boys kept up a running commentary on each other's odors and extrusions, a pair of Sloaney girls whispered excitedly, and, worst of all, a group of Russians gibbered and jabbered until about two in the morning. Finally quiet descended, but not long after this I was awoken by a deafening sound that I initially took to be some kind of wake-up klaxon, but which actually revealed itself to be the honking of geese. (Our section of field was close to a pond.)

I peeked out of my tent, and was confronted with a scene from a Salgado photograph. The dawn mist was rising to reveal a disheveled mass of humanity. Overnight, the queue had carried on expanding and even now there were hundreds of people streaming into the field. It was just after 5 a.m., and everyone was awake. Powered by an energy that emanated more from my surroundings than from anything internal, I put on my clothes and set about disassembling my tent. I cannot remember much about the rest of the morning. All I know is that, having packed up our stuff, we began queuing in earnest. At sluglike pace, we trailed our way down a path that led from the field to a park and eventually crossed over a bridge that ended up in the All-England Club. The whole process took about four hours.

Finally, we arrived at the turnstiles, at which point I spotted Tani, one of the Backpack Babes from Halle. I hadn't spoken to her much in Germany, but we recognized each other, and said hello. She was with a new, unfamiliar group of *RF*-clad women. Tani told me that she'd been camping the whole tournament, spending her days alternately queuing and watching Federer's matches. I could only marvel at such dedication. One night in the open felt like quite enough for me. "What about if he gets to the final?" I asked. "Then we'll have to see," she said.

Federer was first match on Court No. 1 that day. At the turnstile, I was offered a choice of excellent seats, and I plumped for one in the second row behind the server's arm. (I never have quite managed to decide whether it's better to sit directly behind the server or to the side.) Once I'd gained admission, there was more hanging around, as it was only 10 a.m. and play didn't start till one. I found a quiet spot and spent the next three hours to all intents and purposes asleep, save for the fact that I had my eyes open. At some stage, I must have drifted off properly, because the next thing I knew it was ten past one and I was in danger of missing the start of the match. I hurried to the entrance to my section of the stands; the match had indeed just started, and I wouldn't now be able to take my seat until the third game changeover. Standing on tiptoes, I could just about see over the top of the steps and, at the far end of the court, catch sporadic glimpses of the upper half of Federer's body. Next to me a Malaysian-looking man was doing the same. "Well, at least we won't have long to wait," I said.

But he shook his head sadly. "I don't have a ticket. I have traveled all the way here and it is impossible to get any. This is the first time in my life I have ever seen him," he said, nodding towards Federer.

"Haven't you tried camping?" I asked. "That's how I got my ticket."

"What do you mean, camping? You can get tickets that way?" the man asked. "I haven't heard anything about that."

Of course, it immediately occurred to me what I should do: I should hand the man—who was in fact Burmese—my ticket, simply give it to him and head home. But I'm afraid I didn't. Obsession breeds selfishness. Following on the heels of the impulse to be generous came another thought, which was that I'd earned my right to watch Federer, having spent the past twenty-eight hours in a state of extreme discomfort. And though I'd seen Federer many times and would, assuming he won, almost certainly see him again tomorrow, I really wanted to watch this particular match, and if this man was too badly informed to know how hard it was to get Wimbledon tickets, what strategies were required to do so, well then, that was his problem, not mine. And so, when the changeover arrived a few minutes later, I went in and left him standing there, craning his neck. For all I know, he spent the entire match (which, incidentally, Federer won in straight sets) in that position.

3.

If camping is the Wimbledon equivalent of a Butlins holiday, going there on a debenture ticket is, I suppose, more like staying at the Ritz. But actually, convenience aside, I was struck, next day, by how few real advantages it offered. In many ways, the experience compared unfavorably to queuing. Whereas for the Robredo match I got to sit very nearly at the front, our debenture seats were some forty rows back. True, my friend and I got to display our tickets in special purple-ribboned neck wallets that served to advertise our importance; we had access to an exclusive terrace bar where we could choose from the same miserly selection of drinks available throughout the rest of the grounds, and we could eat lunch in a special sit-down restaurant serving indifferent, eye-wateringly pricey food. But had we had to pay for these privileges (which, luckily, we didn't), it would have set us back thousands, even before we'd forked out for the drinks and the food. I don't mean to appear ungrateful—and I certainly wasn't complaining about being able to watch the tennis—but the whole thing seemed to me to be a scam.

Moreover, the atmosphere was not especially convivial. The people in the debs-only areas had a boorish, self-satisfied air. The men seemed to spend most of the time, even while in their seats, checking their mobiles. The women were edgy and overdressed. Snatches of overheard conversation suggested that the general level of tennis knowledge was not high. "Who is this Russian chap, Dimitrov, that Murray's playing? I've never heard of him," one man asked while waiting to take his seat. "Actually, I think he's supposed to be quite good," his wife replied.

The "Russian," who was second on that day (after Simona Halep had thrashed the previous year's women's finalist, Sabine Lisicki), indeed proved good, and, to general incredulity, despatched Murray in straight sets. Then it was Federer against his compatriot Stanislas Wawrinka. Wawrinka came out in the mood that had won him that year's Australian Open. His backhands were lethal. He won the first set 6–4. But Federer didn't panic, and started playing very near his best himself, mixing up his pace and angles, throwing Wawrinka off his rhythm. He gradually got on top and won in four.

Insofar as I'd given the matter any thought, I assumed that that would be it for me and this year's Wimbledon. I certainly had no inkling that I'd be back, four days later, for the final.

chapter seven

A fan's life

1.

On page one of *Lolita*, Vladimir Nabokov's classic study of pedophilic sexual obsession, Humbert Humbert asks, in relation to his underage paramour: "Did she have a precursor?"[1] While I am not suggesting that there are direct parallels between Humbert's proclivities and the fixation that is

---

1. Nabokov, incidentally, was another tennis-fixated writer: after moving to Germany in the 1920s, he supplemented his income by working sporadically as a tennis coach. Later, tennis would inspire some of the best writing in his most famous novel, including this wonderful description of Lolita serving: "She smiled up with gleaming teeth at the small globe suspended so high in the zenith of the powerful and graceful cosmos she had created for the express purpose of falling upon it with a clean resounding crack of her golden whip."

the subject of this book, the question, at least, strikes me as pertinent. A sports fan's enthusiasms, after all, may well be marked by a degree of consistency over the years—a tendency for certain tastes and predilections to be serially in evidence. This, it seems to me, is yet another example of the ways in which the conditions of love and fanship are not dissimilar.

So what has proved to be my sporting type? And to what extent is Federer a match for it? As I've already mentioned, the concept of being a fan meant little to me when I was very young. It was unfathomable, alien. But when I reached the age of twelve or thirteen, this—along with much else—began to change. I now found myself becoming strongly drawn to certain athletes, discovering in myself a capacity for empathetic devotion whose intensity, at least to begin with, took me by surprise. The first sportsman to thus command my affection was the cricketer Allan Lamb. "Lamby," a burly figure with immense forearms, a mustache and a mullet, was a regular in the England teams of the eighties and early nineties. He wasn't an elegant batsman, nor a particularly outstanding one. In Tests, his average languished in the midthirties—well below the top rank. But he had two invaluable qualities: he was good against fast bowling, and he was excellent in one-day matches, where his ability to maneuver the ball around the field—and, occasionally, hit explosive sixes—came into its own. The former attribute was particularly useful during this period, when the West Indies were the dominant cricketing team. England's batting line-ups would habitually crumble in the face of their fearsome pace attacks, and often it would seem as if Lamb alone was capable of holding things together.

I have long regarded my liking for Lamb as a somewhat juvenile aberration, in line with my prepubescent dalliance with Bon Jovi. He doesn't (I like to think) fit the mold of subsequent, more sophisticated, attachments. Now I wonder if, in supporting him, I wasn't unconsciously aping my father's devotion to Jimmy Connors. Lamb, it could be argued, was the Connors of the cricketing world. Like Connors, he was an outsider (he grew up in South Africa, as opposed to the American Midwest). His style was also somewhat heterodox: he tended to play his forward defense with his bat a long way in front of his pad, which explains why he was never much good against spin. Like Connors, he was a combative, bullish character who, one felt, had battled the odds to get where he did. And like Connors, he was notorious for being a hell-raiser. (His exploits with Ian "Beefy" Botham were the stuff of legend in the England dressing room, much as Connors's antics with Ilie "Nasty" Nastase acquired a certain seamy notoriety.) Is it possible that, in becoming his fan, I was paying a complicated homage to my father, channeling his tastes while asserting my independence?

Maybe. In any case, my devotion to Lamb was short-lived. He was soon replaced by a pair of sportsmen whose influence on my adolescence would prove altogether more far-reaching. In fact, it is no exaggeration to say that, pre-Federer, these were my two most significant attachments. Their objects were another cricketer and a snooker player—Graeme Hick and Jimmy White. I first became aware of Hick around 1987. He was Zimbabwean, the son of a tobacco farmer, and had started playing in England—for Worcestershire—while still a teenager. Right away, he showed himself to be a batsman of remarkable promise, a run machine with a seemingly endless capacity to churn out big—sometimes gargantuan—centuries. Zimbabwe, in those days, wasn't a Test-playing nation, though there was talk of it becoming one. In order to give himself the best chance of competing at the highest level, Hick made the pragmatic decision to switch nationalities. He opted to become British, and embarked on a convoluted qualification process that would see him finally make his debut for his adopted county in the summer of 1991, aged twenty-five.

Because English cricket was, in the late eighties, in such a dire state, and because Hick's prequalifying achievements were so impressive, a legend grew up around him during those years. He was to be the savior of our national game, the man who would revive the fortunes of a once-great Test-playing nation. As soon as he had fulfilled his seven-year residency requirements, a new and glorious era for English cricket would begin. For me, that was an immensely exciting prospect. England's regular thrashings at the hands of other countries—most notably the West Indies, but also, from the late eighties onwards, a rejuvenated Australia—were, at the time, a source of anguish to me. England's bowlers were acknowledged to be pretty ineffectual, but it was their frequent, inexplicable batting collapses that bewildered and riled me the most. With Hick in the team, such fragility, I felt certain, would cease. He would provide the much-needed backbone. Indeed, his prodigious run-scoring for his county (1,000 runs before the end of May in 1988, including one innings of 405 not out; an average of more than 90 in 1990) pointed to an impact still more dramatic. Many, back then, saw him as the new Bradman.

So what a letdown it was—and what despair I felt!—when Hick's messianic moment finally arrived, and he utterly failed to bring about the promised transformation. England were playing the West Indies that summer. Hick performed promisingly enough in the one-day internationals, scoring 86 not out in one match, but in the Tests he simply froze. His legs looked as if they'd been shackled in iron. He couldn't handle the West Indians' short balls. He barely seemed capable of hitting a boundary, let alone constructing a substantial innings. Each effortful occupation of the crease ended in the same dismal fashion. After four Tests, he averaged just ten, whereupon he was dropped—something that was to prove a regular occurrence.

It was horrible, watching Hick fail like this. And he continued to fail during England's next few series. Eventually, matters improved somewhat. Hick scored his maiden Test century, against India, early in 1993, and for the next few seasons performed credibly—if not outstandingly—as an England batsman, doing particularly well in one-day internationals. But then, in the second half of the decade, his Test form deserted him again, and from then on he was regarded primarily as a limited overs specialist. For a batsman of his supposed abilities, what a comedown that must have been, to find himself edged out of Test contention by players who, early in their careers, hadn't been thought of as having a fraction of his talent. He remained a bit-part player for England until 2001, whereupon he was excised from the team one last time. He ended his Test career with an average of 31.32, which, for a man who played as many matches as he did—sixty-five—is almost embarrassingly low.

I remember being hugely puzzled by it, this disparity between Hick's potential—as evidenced by his early achievements—and his failure to perform when playing for England. What was the source of the problem? Was it technical or psychological? Various theories were advanced. Some said that Hick was technically suspect against the short ball—that he didn't move his feet properly—and that this flaw, which for the most part went unexploited by mediocre county attacks, proved crippling against the more penetrating bowlers he encountered at Test level. I never entirely bought this theory. Most players have small flaws, or stylistic idiosyncrasies, and if they are good—as Hick undoubtedly was—they iron them out, or find a way to succeed in spite of them. And it's not as if Hick didn't face—and score runs against—genuinely world-class bowlers early in his career. In 1988, for Worcestershire, needing another 153 runs to complete the milestone of 1,000 runs before the end of May, and with only one match left, he scored 172 against a touring West Indies side whose attack included Courtney Walsh, Curtly Ambrose, and Ian Bishop. Besides, there were plenty of excellent bowlers in county cricket.

Hick's main problem, I believe, was psychological, and sprang from the interaction between the tendencies of his temperament and the unusual circumstances of his career. Something about the artificiality of his extended apprenticeship for Test cricket, and the pressure that must have built up during that time, evidently got to him. When he finally came to play for England, his mind-set was such that he simply couldn't be the confident, bullying shot-maker he was for his country. He became tentative, shackled. His choice of adopted country, I'm sure, exacerbated the problem. The combination of self-doubt and grandiosity that defined England's sporting mind-set at this time—a mind-set that, recently, has shown encouraging signs of becoming more balanced—caused Hick to be saddled with ridiculous expectations. He wasn't allowed to be merely an exciting prospect: upon his shoulders rested the task of transforming the cricketing fortunes of an entire nation. Some might not have found this an intolerable burden, but Hick—who never struck me as a particularly carefree character, who in fact seemed to be naturally given to self-doubt—evidently did.

And I found it painful to contemplate, the effect all this must have had on the psyche of a man who, one sensed, wasn't well set up to cope with adversity. Because he had enjoyed such spectacular early success—because he had never had to struggle—it seemed likely that, when he did find himself under real pressure, he would have few resources to draw upon. He was a big man with a quiet, solitary air—a gentle giant. He never looked entirely at ease amid the rough-and-tumble, the backslapping camaraderie, of team life. He was, one felt, a silent sufferer, a bottler-upper—not someone who could shrug off disappointment. Unlike Lamb—a very different type of outsider—there was nothing cocky about him. His roots hadn't emboldened him, but had made him awkward, hesitant. Playing for England, he never looked like he truly believed he belonged. When trudging off the field after yet another failure, his face wouldn't register anger or frustration, but would express, instead, a kind of baffled resignation. He would often slowly let his eyes fall shut—always, for me, an intensely moving sight.

In Hick's story, I came to feel, was a morality tale about a certain kind of overreach. Ambition is fine, but it's not for everyone. It was a mistake for Hick to have switched nationalities. He should have sat it out and waited for Zimbabwe to achieve Test status. The irony is that his Test debut would only have come one year later than it did: Zimbabwe played its first Test—against India—in 1992. Naturally, this is speculation, but my belief is that, had Hick stuck with the land of his birth, he would have achieved far greater success as a Test batsman than he did.

2.

My other sporting hero during my teens, Jimmy White, was also a paragon of epic underachievement. His problem was, in a way, more straightforward than Hick's. Certainly it was easier to diagnose. White was an attacking, fast-playing genius of the type that snooker seems to throw up every fifteen years or so; the other two examples during my lifetime have been Alex Higgins and Ronnie O'Sullivan. And as with both of them, White's genius was laced through with vulnerability, to the extent that the two seemed inseparable. A South Londoner, he had spent his childhood playing truant from school, hanging out at Zan's snooker hall in Tooting, lightening the wallets of older opponents. This artificially lit boyhood—combined with an adult taste for revelry—left its mark in a livid white-red pallor. He became world amateur champion aged eighteen. No player has ever been more attractive to watch, communicated such free-flowing ease. And he was lovable, too, with his Cockney cadences, his air of high-spirited abandon. The crowds adored him.

Yet White had problems that went beyond drinking, gambling, and drug-taking—the standard peccadilloes among players of the time. His real failing was a suspect temperament. Under pressure, he had a tendency to fall to pieces. I first became aware of this right at the start of my snooker-watching life, in 1985, when White met Cliff Thorburn in the final of a second-tier tournament called the Matchroom Trophy. The match was best of twenty-three frames, and after the first session White led 7–0, having played what one of the commentators described as "perfect snooker." In the first frame of the second session, he carried on where he left off, hitting a break that left Thorburn needing four snookers. But then he got careless; he gave away a string of easy fouls; Thorburn clinched the frame. And from this point, it was a different story. White's focus and confidence evaporated and Thorburn—whose nickname was "The Grinder"—battled his way to an improbable 12–10 victory. I remember feeling pretty distraught.

White's weakness under pressure would repeatedly prove his undoing in snooker's biggest tournament, and the one that mattered most to him: the World Championship. He reached the final six times, including five times consecutively between 1990 and 1994. On four of those occasions he faced Stephen Hendry, the dominant player of the nineties, and arguably the best of all time. Hendry was a ruthless, icy Scot—temperamentally, the antithesis of White. And yet White really should have beaten him in two of their meetings. In 1992, playing superbly, he led 12–6 and 14–8. Then he got nervous, started missing shots he normally would have made blindfolded, let Hendry back in. The Scot won ten straight frames to take the title 18–14. Two years later, even more agonizingly, their match went to a final-frame decider. In among the balls, and with only a few more pots needed, White twitched on a straightforward black, once again handing victory to Hendry.

There was, about these losses, a certain horrible inevitability—the sense of a deeply ingrained flaw inexorably reasserting itself, even when conditions seemed ideal for it to be overcome. White often struck me as being a bit like an addict who never quite manages to rid himself of his vices, always succumbing at the final hurdle. And what made his failure to win the World Snooker Championship all the sadder was that he evidently cared so much. As he freely admitted, winning the title—just once—was his life's ambition. Yet he never managed it.

I, too, experienced a searing pain at those defeats, a plangent misery that lasted for days. It was a pain based partly on sympathy for White, but also on a larger sense that an injustice had been perpetrated. White represented something for me—and, I don't doubt, for countless others—that was closely tied to the visual appeal of his game. Quite simply, he made a sport not known for its aesthetic qualities wonderful to behold. When he was in full flow, the balls span and clashed to his whim; every rebound, every kiss, appeared deliberate, intricately contrived. I have always had a sense—though I wouldn't have been able to articulate it when younger—that beauty, in sport, confers its own entitlement. It *should* trump the more workaday qualities of consistency, ruthlessness, strength. The fact that, in White's case, it so clearly didn't instilled in me a certain pessimism about the possibilities for beauty in sport, a belief that, where it existed, there was also likely to be fragility, vulnerability. The kind of talent that White embodied—an unusually pure kind, one that expressed itself as instinct—I came to associate with ineffectuality. And this paralleled something I'd come to believe about tennis, which is that, in the modern era, beauty was being remorselessly edged out.

3.

Of course, precursors are never exact predictors. Sporting infatuations, no less than romantic ones, have an aspect of the unfathomable. Part of their point is that they cannot easily be accounted for, neatly slotted into an overarching narrative. The lines leading from Hick and White to Federer are by no means straight. Yet there are enough echoes and overlaps to suggest that there has been a logic, a teleology of sorts, to the patterning of my enthusiasms. Like Hick,

Federer achieved phenomenal success relatively early in his career, and appeared to have no weaknesses. And yet, when the really big tests came, he failed to live up to expectations. Like Hick, he displayed, on those all-important occasions, a certain tactical—and psychological—brittleness, a sense of being unwilling, or unable, to change. He appeared baffled, confounded. Like White, Federer regularly lost the grueling battles with the most iron-willed of his opponents. Like White, he stands—for me and many others—as a powerful emblem of the seductive power of natural talent and beauty, qualities that, in the modern era, seem increasingly fragile, ever more imminently under threat.

Moreover, with all three athletes, there was—is—a marked gap between possibility and attainment, ideal and reality. And this gap is the source of the pathos I associate with them. Federer, it's true, has objectively been far more successful than either Hick or White, and so it might seem perverse to insist that he, too, hasn't lived up to expectations, that the same aura of underachievement clings to him. Yet it needs to be remembered that, in Federer's case, the ideals were more exalted. White wanted to win the World Snooker Championship; Hick wanted to be a successful English batsman (or, in the end, just to play for England); what was possible for Federer at one point seemed limitless. Call it insatiability, call it greed, but when perfection is what you're striving for, and what you once had, then the knife of disappointment cuts no less sharply, only at a different point. Records become markers not of fulfillment but of a kind of failure, testaments to all that hasn't been achieved. In such circumstances, what limits can be placed on ambition? Why should seventeen grand slams be enough?

Success, in sport as in life, is always relative. To gauge what it means, you have to understand what it's being measured against. When the defeats come, the proceeding triumphs evaporate: it's as if they'd never existed, had only ever been dreams. For the fan, a balanced reckoning of positive and negative is never achievable. When failure and disappointment come—as they inevitably will—they always hurt just the same.

4.

How all-encompassing has my devotion to Federer been? In practical terms, it has certainly had a substantial impact on my life. I've spent an awful lot of time watching—and rewatching—his matches, rising frequently in the middle of the night to do so. Countless additional hours have been spent studying home-curated YouTube collections of his greatest shots, or eye-level videos of his practices, or reading the things, both positive and negative, that people have written about him in obscure corners of the Internet. And because I've spent so much time doing all this, there are lots of other things that I haven't done, things that might be said to have more inherent value, such as reading books or earning money or putting washes on or having sex, things that—had I done them—might have caused me to be regarded, and to regard myself, as a more successful, rounded person.

Yet I'm not sure that any of this really matters. I wouldn't want to be the kind of person whose entire life was dedicated to making efficient use of his time. A meaningful existence, for me, is one in which meaninglessness has room to flourish. One of the qualities I am least drawn to in other people is an overriding sense of purpose. There are lots of hours in the day, lots of days in the year, and time can always be found, even if it can't be regained. There is no part of me that begrudges the hours, the years, I've spent watching Federer, although others—my wife included—might have something to say about this.

The more important question, I think, is psychological. Part of me, these last several years, has always, in some sense, been attached to him. We have had a relationship of sorts— albeit an unusually asymmetrical one. (I know a great deal about him; so far, he's maintained his complete ignorance of me.) So the issue is really this: How much has that investment compromised my ability to give of myself in other ways? Or, to put the matter more generally: Do the feelings fans experience cut into, or lessen, the feelings they have available in other parts of their lives, to give to the people they actually know? Does the one kind of love cannibalize the other?

I don't know if there's a straightforward answer to this question. It goes without saying that there is something irrational about fanship, and that, taken to extremes, it can become delusory, unhinged. But then anything, practiced to excess, has baleful consequences. You can be obsessed by the meaning of life, or by the germs that reside in the pores of your skin, and in either case, if the preoccupation hinders your ability to function, you need to get yourself to a head doctor. There are fans who manage to keep their attachments in check, and others who take them way too far. I'm not sure that any of the problems that result should be laid entirely at the door of fanship.

On the other hand, there is something about being a fan that seems to go with obsessiveness—and Federer fans are especially susceptible on this front. Over the last few years, I've encountered a number of other ardent Fedheads, quite a few of whom have exhibited an extremity of devotion that makes my own pretensions to loyalty feel lightweight, fraudulent. Take, for instance, my Polish friend Mike, whom I first met six years ago on some public courts in Camberwell. I was alone, practicing my serve, which has always been the big weakness of my game, when Mike walked up and asked if I wanted a hit. He immediately stood out from the court's other regular users, who tended towards scrappiness both in dress and technique. Mike was exclusively—and expensively—kitted out in *RF*-branded clothing. He opened his red Wilson holdall to reveal six 90-square-inch Wilsons. "I have every model Roger has ever used in here," he said. Even his string tensions, he explained, were identical to the maestro's: "Forty-eight on the mains, forty-five on the crosses." He could have been about to turn up to play at Wimbledon.

Mike told me that he had only been playing for three years, and was entirely self-taught. We started hitting, and two things became clear. First, for someone who'd played the game for such a short time, he was remarkably good. Second, his style was uncannily familiar. He had taught himself to play, he said, by standing, racket in hand, in front of slow-motion videos of Federer, shadowing his movements, and he had memorized every last detail of his idol's game. It was all there: the high, economical takeback on the forehand, the decisive planting of the right foot just prior to hitting the backhand, the distinctive head dip and lean-in of the body when moving forward for a short ball. His game was a faithful facsimile, a pure testament of devotion, and the result was that playing him felt a bit like facing Federer himself—albeit a version that I could beat.

At least, I thought I could beat Mike, but I've never been completely sure. Over the next couple of years, Mike and I arranged to play every couple of weeks—although play isn't really the right word, because Mike only ever wanted to knock up. He told me that he'd often spend five or six hours a day just doing that. At first this puzzled me: isn't the competitive challenge of tennis the sport's main point? What is the good of practicing if you never actually play? But I grew to understand that, for Mike, tennis wasn't about winning and losing. All he wanted to do was hit balls and, by doing so, get his shots just right. And what getting his shots right meant, of course, was getting them just like Federer's. Identifying with Federer—in a sense, *becoming* him—was, for Mike, the whole attraction.

One day, Mike turned up with his two-and-a-half-year-old son in tow—his wife was busy, he explained. I didn't know that he had a son, and so asked what his name was.

Mike looked at me askance for a moment, as if I'd said something incredibly stupid. And before the answer left his lips, I knew what it would be. Roger was deposited on a chair by the side of the court, adjacent to the net, and was told by his father to sit still. For about half an hour, he stayed in place, playing the part of mute umpire. (I had the sense that he'd done this before.) Then he got bored and began roaming around the side of the court, placing himself in the path of mishit balls. Mike apologized and said he had to go.

Roger had been born, I subsequently learned, on August 10—two days after Federer's birthday. This, Mike freely admitted, was no accident. The conception had been carefully orchestrated. And nothing was supposed to have been left to chance. The plan, Mike told me, had been to have a caesarean on the eighth. Except he and his wife had chosen the wrong year. The eighth fell on a Saturday—when the hospital didn't offer elective cesareans. "I did everything to bring it on," Mike told me. "I cooked her the most powerful curry ever." But it hadn't worked, and Roger's birthday was sadly out of whack.

Another time, one November, when I was at work, Mike called me. "Do you want to see Roger play Mardy Fish at the O2 this afternoon?" he asked. "I have a spare ticket." He explained that he, Roger, and his wife had been planning to go, but his wife had had to pull out at the last minute. I hesitated for a moment—things were quite busy that day—but, unable to resist, I agreed. I met Mike and Roger outside the arena shortly before two o'clock. Our seats were pretty good—about twenty rows back, behind the server's arm. But they weren't good enough for Mike. As soon as the match started, he began anxiously scanning the rows in front of us, checking for vacated seats. Every time one became available, he would say: "Come on, let's get it." Thus, over the next hour, the three of us descended disjointedly through the crowd, eventually making our way to the very front. At this point, Mike pulled from his bag an immensely long-lensed camera—a pap's camera—and began taking photos, not just of Federer but also of Mirka and his parents, Lynette and Robert, who were sitting, also in the front row, about twenty meters away. It was a long match—it went to three sets—and towards the end, Roger Jr. again grew restless, and began roaming along the row, making little bids for freedom. If Mike was taking photos, I would have to hurry off and retrieve him. It was an oddly stressful way to watch a tennis match.

Mike and I would endlessly talk about Federer, but precious little else. To this day—and I still occasionally hit with him—I know little about him: what his wife thinks about his obsession, how he gets the money to fund it, what it really means. He is a mystery to me. All I know is that he is an extreme embodiment of a particular approach to fanship, one whose entire basis is imitative, replicatory. It is clear to me that Mike (whose fanatical tendencies, I should emphasize, don't prevent him from being an extremely nice person) wants to *be* Federer, and, insofar as this can be achieved, he has arranged his life to make the fantasy real.

5.

Federer's female fans, not altogether surprisingly, don't want to be him. But they are no less passionate in their devotion. In fact, in my experience, women are much more likely to follow Federer, in the literal sense of traveling across the world to watch him. You see the Backpack Babes, or groups like them, in the stands wherever he plays. More often than not, those red-and-white clusters are made up entirely of women.

It seems to me that, for many such women, Federer likewise functions as a fantasy object. He is a kind of ideal man—although the precise form the fantasy takes varies. Sexual attraction has something to do with it—his female fans routinely comment on his sexiness and good looks and excitedly swap photos of him changing his shirt or lounging on the beach—but it's more than just this. Certain women, it seems to me, are drawn to Federer precisely because the sexuality he embodies is a restrained, partially submerged one. A large part of his appeal is rooted in the fact that his persona embraces other, less stereotypically "male" qualities.

What kind of "ideal man" is Federer? I've noticed three distinct archetypes, although no doubt there are others. One is a view of him that emphasizes his caring side—his softness and compassion. You could call this version Federer the saint. His fans often talk about him in a way that imputes to him almost superhuman qualities of empathy and understanding. They say things like: "He is so intuitive. He always wants to take care of us, to know that we're all right." Sometimes, he is credited with almost Jesus-like powers. At Wimbledon, I met a woman with an arthritic condition that causes her hands to be blistered and painful. She told me about once meeting Federer. "He was so gentle with me, the way he took my hands. He understood immediately how sensitive they were, and treated me with special care." She didn't quite say that, after he'd touched them, her hands miraculously felt better, but had she done so, I wouldn't have been entirely surprised.

Another Federer archetype is that of the perfect life partner, the ideal husband. In this version, the qualities he is most admired for are the way he circumnavigates difficulty, deals with pressure, and fits so much in. Federer, famously, always appears relaxed and gives the impression of being able to effortlessly flit between his various roles—those of athlete, family man, celebrity, and philanthropist. In this sense, he is the ideal of a certain kind of modern masculinity, one that celebrates capability, all-roundedness. This is not the most romantic view of Federer; you could say it's more of a practical one. One woman I spoke to at the World Tour Finals, a policy expert from Bangladesh who had come all the way to London on her own just to watch Federer, seemed to see him very much in these terms: she spoke admiringly of how he managed to combine his work and his family commitments, of the impressive "balance" that he managed to strike. It was almost as if she were describing a successful CEO. Yet I was also struck by the discrepancy between the measured way she talked about Federer to me and the far more passionate, breathless tone of her (anonymous) Twitter feed.

The third ideal of Federer is highly romantic. In this

version, he is, more than anything else, an artistic figure—a kind of creative genius. This was very much how Marcia—the Brazilian woman I met on the train at Halle—saw him. Subsequently, via email, I discovered more about her life. Her background is in theater: she worked for many years as an actress at the Théâtre du Soleil in Paris—an avant-garde company founded by Ariane Mnouchkine—and she said that she always saw the similarities between tennis and theater. Her life, as she described it to me, had been a shifting, nomadic one; she could have been a character in a Bolaño novel. In the late 1960s, Marcia had fought against the military dictatorship in Brazil, and had been imprisoned for a year and a half. After that, she had been a political exile for twenty years, living in Chile, Argentina, Denmark, Portugal, and France. She had been married to a Brazilian writer, then later had lived with a Chilean writer and composer. She returned to Brazil in 1994 and, soon after that, started working for the Brazilian embassy in Vietnam, overseeing the cultural relations between the two countries. In Vietnam, she couldn't initially watch tennis, but finally got cable at her house in 2008. It was then, at the French Open, that she first saw Federer. She was, she told me, "absolutely moved," and since then has followed him passionately. It was as if, for her, he represented an ideal of artistic beauty that she had been chasing her whole life.

So, three very different, even contradictory archetypes: Federer the saint, the modern husband, and the artistic genius. Perhaps the fact that Federer can plausibly be all three is in itself revealing, for it points to another of his qualities, which is a kind of plasticity, an ability to fit whatever fantasy is projected upon him. There's a sense, with Federer, that his image is ever-shifting; he can be whatever you want him to be.

6.

What about for me? What element of my own personality does Federer speak to? What fantasy does he embody? I have often wondered about this, and I've come to the conclusion that there are a few different things. Of course, the fact that Federer's tennis is so attractive is, for me, a huge part of his appeal. Like Marcia, I have always been drawn to beauty, especially in sport, and Federer, in lots of ways, represents an aesthetic ideal. But there are other factors. Timing is significant. I became obsessed with Federer at a point when I was emerging from the depression that had dominated my life for several years, and he was somehow integral to my recovery. I was, during this period, coming to understand myself, and my past, in a new way. I was trying to reconcile the divisions within me that had led me to have no real idea who I was—sporty or intellectual, a thinking person or a feeling one. As I saw it, Federer was someone who had reconciled the divergent tendencies within tennis—between power and grace, modernity and tradition—and, in doing so, had enabled the sport to arrive at a kind of rapprochement with its own past. What had been in conflict, he yoked back together. I, too, was searching for a way back to the sources of good, of life, within me. There was a corollary, I felt, between what Federer had achieved in the context of tennis and what I needed to bring about within myself.

But as well as being a reconciling figure, Federer also embodies, for me, the idea of something lost, an idyll that cannot be retrieved. Even while he managed to forge a link with the past through his playing style and his personality, he became a kind of exile from his own history, from the boundless promise of his years of dominance. This idea of a golden era that cannot be recaptured, or an ideal that cannot be lived up to, has always resonated with me. I don't know quite why this is; maybe it relates, again, to the idea of some part of myself being lost. More generally, perhaps, it is a metaphor for childhood. We can remember our childhoods, but we can never go back to them. Life's progress, life's increase, inevitably brings with it a diminishment, a falling away.

Federer once told an interviewer that he never looks back, doesn't dwell on past mistakes and misfortunes, only ever looks forward. No doubt, that's a useful—probably essential—mindset for a top athlete. But for me, Federer has always been a backward-facing figure, someone defined by his relationship with the past. Thanks to him, I have sometimes felt as if I've been able to live my life over, to make sense of all that went wrong, and, as a result, to be a happier, freer adult. I wouldn't go so far as to say that my obsession with Federer saved me, but it has certainly brought me a tremendous amount of happiness.

Sunday, July 6, 2014 (continued)

As Federer and Djokovic knock up, I think back to some of their previous encounters. In big tournaments, their matches have generally been close. It's as if their games are a good fit, a good marriage; they don't negate but spur each other on. Over recent years, they have had some truly epic contests: those consecutive, weirdly similar US Open semifinals in 2010 and 2011, with the double match points relinquished by Federer in both; that sublime four-set semifinal win at Roland Garros in 2011, ending Djokovic's winning run; the spellbinding WTF final in 2012, with its staggering passing shots. Although Federer struggles to beat Djokovic—and in fact, these days, more often than not loses to him—there's not a sense, as with Nadal, that he recoils from playing the

Serb. Djokovic doesn't blunt him, reduce him, as the Spaniard does; his game doesn't hold the same terrors.

I think, too, about how strange it feels to be here, at an actual Wimbledon final. For virtually my whole life, this has seemed an unreachable ambition. I've never pictured myself attending one, certainly not one involving Federer. I have a clear memory of one sweltering July afternoon when I was seven, going to the house of my piano teacher. She was hosting an end-of-year get-together for her students. One arrived much later than everyone else. He was Chinese, the son of a well-known violinist. He was late, he let slip, because he'd just come from Wimbledon, where, with his parents, he'd watched McEnroe dispose of Connors in one of the most one-sided men's finals ever.[2] Now, as I sit in my seat up in the rafters, I think back to that moment, and remember how astonished I'd been at the good fortune of this boy, upon whom had been bestowed, it seemed to me, the keys to paradise.

And I wonder: what kind of final will this one prove to be? It seems almost unthinkable that it could be great, like 2008—or indeed like 2007 or 2009. I'm not even sure I'd want it to be. I doubt my capacity to handle the tension. In many ways, I'd prefer it to be one-sided, more like 1984. But that's a stupid thought, really, because if it's one-sided, Federer will almost certainly lose. He is never going to beat Djokovic in straight sets, although Djokovic could easily beat him in three. If Federer is to have a chance of winning, he will

---

2. McEnroe, playing perhaps the best tennis of his career, had beaten his rival 6–1, 6–1, 6–2.

have to do it the hard way—in unbearable, drawn-out fashion. Whatever happens, the next few hours will be difficult.

To begin with, however, things are even, predictable. Both players hold their serves comfortably. They are striking the ball well, carrying on their good form from previous rounds. Federer is serving superbly, as he has throughout the tournament. This is a hopeful sign: he has no chance of beating Djokovic if he doesn't serve well, because Djokovic is the best returner in the world. But this, on its own, is not enough. Djokovic, at some stage, will undoubtedly break him. To win, he also has to apply pressure when Djokovic is serving, to attack him, force the issue. And here, early on, things look less promising. Djokovic, for the most part, holds serve comfortably.

The first set goes to a tiebreak. Federer starts it well, goes a break up, but then lets the advantage slip. Djokovic edges ahead. And he gets a minibreak to bring up a set point on his serve. It already feels as if Federer is on the precipice. To have any sort of chance, he surely *has* to win this set. A nervy exchange follows, a Federer forehand looks as if it's going out but lands right in the corner, produces a Djokovic error. Federer goes down set point a second time, this time saves it with an ace, and then, unexpectedly, Djokovic nets a relatively simple backhand to hand Federer the set. My relief is immense, but I still don't feel as if anything very solid has been achieved. Djokovic will surely come back stronger.

And indeed, he does. Over the next two and a half hours, a horror show unfolds. It is not that Federer is playing badly—he is still serving well—but Djokovic has him in a kind of grip.

The problem stems, to a large extent, from the Serb's serve. Federer just can't make any impression on it. Commentators often describe Federer's serve as underrated, but Djokovic's is, I think, even more so. It's not a spectacular shot—he doesn't hit many aces—but his first serve is hard and well disguised, and his second serve is almost impossible to attack. Ever since he adjusted his action around 2010, he has been able to put a quite phenomenal degree of spin on his second delivery, and now, on this sun-hardened surface, you can see very clearly the way the ball (almost always hit to the backhand), leaps up high, around Federer's ears. He is struggling to do anything with it, anything at all, and Djokovic is invariably getting up in the rally—an advantage he seldom relinquishes.

During the first three sets, Federer brings up just a solitary break point—which he fails to take. Djokovic doesn't do much better—he gets just three—but he takes one of them in the second set, which enables him to win it. The third set, like the first, goes to a tiebreak; this time, Federer falters, misfires on a couple of forehands. Suddenly he's two sets to one down. This is unbearably depressing. The movement of the match seems to be all in one direction; Federer is gradually being edged out, smothered not by brilliance but by Djokovic's relentlessness, his metronomic shot making, his consistency. In virtually every department—apart from in aces—Federer is coming off just a little bit worse. Towards the end of the third set, he changes his tactics, starts chipping the ball, and rushing to the net on virtually every point, but even that makes no difference: unerringly, Djokovic strokes the ball past him every time.

When the third set ends, I leave the stadium, head to the toilet, and, for a moment, feel tempted to stay there. I don't want to see any more of this. I am not having a good time. When Federer took the first set, I momentarily felt hopeful, but since then everything has been ghastly. I never—obviously—like to see Federer lose, but I particularly hate it when I feel he hasn't had an opportunity to really play his game, to express himself. Should he lose in four sets—which is now looking highly likely—I know that I will be consumed by frustration, and will return home feeling profoundly miserable. Of course, the thought of how much my ticket cost only makes it worse: so much money wasted!

Near the start of the fourth set, Federer is broken. This time—for the first time in the match—he breaks back, but next game Djokovic breaks *again*, and moves into a 5–2 lead. There is surely no escape for Federer now. His first Grand Slam final for two years—in all probability his last one ever—is going to end up being no sort of contest. By now the crowd is morose, dejected. Virtually everyone, apart from the woman sitting immediately in front of me, who keeps screaming out "Go on, Nole!" wants Federer to rally, to make a match of it. We are all desperate for something—anything—to happen.

And then, at the very last moment, it does. With Djokovic serving for the match, Federer, as if from nowhere, finds a new focus, a new energy. He is helped a bit by nervousness on Djokovic's part—the Serb sprays an easy forehand long at the start of the game—but the two points that Federer plays from 30–all have nothing to do with his opponent's nerves and everything to do with his own tenacity, his determination to stay alive. A savage crosscourt backhand brings up break point, and then a swooping, on-the-run forehand, hit down the line with incredible whip, brings him the game. He faces a match point in his next service game, and saves it with an ace. Then he breaks Djokovic again, and holds serve to force a fifth set.

This passage of play—in which Federer reels off five consecutive games—probably takes all of twenty minutes. But those twenty minutes are among the most ecstatic of my Federer-watching life. Every point he wins, I—along with a few other people (overwhelmingly men) dotted around my section of the crowd—simultaneously rise to our feet, pump our fists, make demented eye contact with each other. We cannot help it. What was improbable—impossible—seems to be coming to pass. Federer is turning this around.

I have never been a tribal fan, never a banner waver. I have never felt particularly at home in groups, or in crowds. My devotion to Federer has been overwhelmingly a personal, inward-facing thing. But right now I am part of something, part of the energy, the collective will, that is sweeping through the crowd, and buoying Federer up, injecting an unforeseen sprightliness into his ageing legs. And it feels wonderful. I want this to go on and on.

In the final set, for a game or two, it does. Djokovic looks tired, deflated; Federer carries on looking energized. But then—almost inevitably—Djokovic steels himself once more. His rhythm returns. Gradually, he reassumes control. And Federer—as is his tendency these days, at the end of long matches—falls away a bit, loses his consistency. At 4–4, 15–all, on Djokovic's serve, he misses a smash. It's as if that is the moment when his belief finally fades. He loses the game, and then gets broken, spraying errors all over the place. Djokovic sinks to grounds, bites a bit of the turf.

The presentations and speeches happen very quickly. After the open-endedness of the match, there's a sense of order hastily being restored, or ceremony taking over. Federer gives a simple, brief speech. His daughters, Myla and Charlene, in identical spotty dresses, sit on the railings at the front of the players' section, dangling their legs off the edge. I realize that I'm not quite as upset as I'd assumed I would be. Somehow, the fact that Federer pulled things round in the fourth set, that he at least rallied, made his eventual loss easier to bear.

I leave the auditorium and head to Henman Hill, wondering if Tani, or anyone else I know, will be there. Marcia had mentioned that, should Federer reach the final, she would try and come over from Paris (although I later learn that flu kept her away). I find Tani with her small band of fellow fans, looking predictably forlorn. Tani suggests that we head over to Centre Court and stand beneath the concourse that runs across to the media center. From there, she says, we'll almost certainly catch a glimpse of Federer, when he walks across to give his press conference. A large crowd has already gathered, and we stand at its edge, about fifty meters from the concourse. We discuss the final. Everyone agrees that it was a bad loss, but not a crushing one. Federer didn't deserve to win today. For most of the match, he wasn't quite good enough. Nor is there a huge animus towards Djokovic. "We don't mind Novak," one woman tells me. "He's done the most to stop Nadal getting close to seventeen."

Djokovic walks out on to the concourse, everyone cheers, and the Serb takes a can of tennis balls, signs them, and starts hurling them into the crowd. With little apparent effort, he sends the balls arcing immensely high and deep. Then he disappears into the media center. "Federer will come out soon, I know he will," Tani says. We wait for another half hour or so. I begin to wonder if I should slope off. But then, finally, Federer does appear, accompanied by one of his daughters—whether Charlene or Myla, it isn't clear. He stands for a few seconds, waves to the crowd, and then turns. For a second, he seems to look straight at our little group, before giving one final wave.

"He saw us!" one of our group says. "He waved right at us."

"No," someone else says. "I think he was just waving in our general direction."

"No," Tani declares. "He was *definitely* waving at us. I know he was. He wanted to thank us for coming, for being here."

And it does seem possible, at this moment, that Federer had indeed spotted the little red-and-white enclave on the fringes of the crowd, and had purposefully singled us out. Suddenly, I feel much better. This really isn't so bad; I can take it. Federer's losses have always cut me to the quick, at times have made me virtually inconsolable, but today, for the first time, it seems enough that I—we—had that magical half hour, when the past once more intruded upon the present, and beauty poured forth, and when everything again seemed possible.

Afterword

Since I finished *Federer and Me*, in late 2014, two things have happened. First, Federer's resurgence has continued. In 2015, he had another very good year, winning 85 percent of his matches (a success rate only fractionally lower than in 2014), claiming six tournaments (as against five the previous year, discounting the Davis Cup), and again coming tantalizingly close to winning an eighteenth major. He continued to play attacking, all-court tennis and even added a brazen new net-rushing tactic, the SABR, to his repertoire. He finished the year ranked three in the world, on the heels of Andy Murray. Retirement looks a distant prospect.

The other thing is that Nadal's fortunes have undergone a dramatic reversal. By his standards, the last twelve months have been abysmal. While it would be foolish to write him off completely (and there have been hints, just recently, that his form is returning), he no longer looks the player he was. Part of me feels pleased about this: I find it funny to think that the displaced monarch may yet outlast the man who overthrew him. It would give Federer a victory of sorts, of a "having the final say" type. Aside from anything else, it plainly demonstrates that Nadal has paid a price for playing the way he does. At twenty-nine, he looks old and spent, whereas Federer, five years his senior, remains ebullient, age-defying.

Yet there's another part of me that feels sorry for the Spaniard. Funnily enough, I find that the worse things get for him, the less objectionable he becomes. He wears adversity well. Nadal has never complained about the diminishment of his powers, never appeared petulant or bitter. "If this is it for me, then so be it," seems to be his creed. In this changed context, the humility that has always come so naturally to him is endearing, although I dare say my fondness would rapidly dissipate were he to become a contender again.

As for Federer, I remain in thrall to him, though perhaps a bit less so than formerly. These days, I don't get quite so upset when he loses. The truth is that I no longer expect him to win, or not the really big matches anyway. And I'm not sure he expects to win them either. That makes things a lot easier for both of us. Being the world's second or third best player in your midthirties, in a position to pounce should Djokovic ever slip up, isn't a bad state of affairs, all told. Certainly, it's one I think I can live with.

November 30, 2015

Acknowledgments

I would like to thank my agent, David Godwin, who (though he may not recall doing so) was the first person to suggest turning my Federer obsession into a book.

Also my editors, Matt Phillips and Justine Taylor: Matt for seizing on the idea and for being exceptionally patient, Justine for being unflaggingly thoughtful and calm.

Various people have talked to me, informally and formally, about Federer, or about the book more generally, and I would like to thank them. They are: Joseph Epstein, Márcia Savaget Fiani, John Yandell, Stephen Mumford, Rod Cross, Benjamin Markovits, Joel Drucker, Tom Perrotta, Richard Moore, Simon Cambers, Ishita Islam, Alexander Regier, Rosalind Porter. I would also like to thank various editors who have published pieces by me on tennis: Thomas Jones, Jane Ferguson, Dan Rosenheck.

ACKNOWLEDGMENTS

I owe a huge debt of gratitude to my parents, Robert and Gus, and to my brother and sister, Edward and Juliet. They have all contributed to this book in numerous, unquantifiable ways.

I would like to thank Monica Steuerman, who helped in a way no one else could.

Finally, I would like to thank my wife, Gudrun, who has not merely put up with my Federer obsession these past few years, but has tolerated the intensification—the layering of one form of obsessiveness over another—that actually writing the thing entailed. Moreover, her editorial advice has, throughout, been crucial. It is hard for me to express how grateful I am.

Bibliography

Books

Auster, Paul, and J. M. Coetzee, *Here and Now: Letters, 2008–2011* (London: Harvill Secker, 2013).

Bowers, Chris, *Roger Federer: The Greatest* (London: John Blake, 2011).

Connors, Jimmy, *The Outsider: My Autobiography* (London: Bantam Press, 2013).

Gallwey, W. Timothy, *The Inner Game of Tennis* (London: Jonathan Cape, 1975).

McPhee, John, *The Levels of the Game* (New York: Farrar Straus Giroux, 1979).

Mumford, Stephen, *Watching Sport: Aesthetics, Ethics and Emotions* (London: Routledge, 2013).

Nadal, Rafael, *Rafa: My Story* (London: Sphere, 2011).

Scruton, Roger, *Beauty* (Oxford: Oxford University Press, 2009).

Wallace, David Foster, *Both Flesh and Not: Essays* (London: Penguin, 2012).

Wertheim, L. Jon, *Strokes of Genius: Federer v Nadal, Rivals in Greatness* (London: JR Books, 2009).

Wilson, Elizabeth, *Love Game: A History of Tennis, from Victorian Pastime to Global Phenomenon* (London: Serpent's Tail, 2014).

Articles

Cross, Rod, "The Inch That Changed Tennis Forever," *Tennis Industry* (January 2006).

Epstein, Joseph, "How Roger Federer Lost his Topspin," *Newsweek* (April 17, 2009).

Markovits, Benjamin, "Disliking Federer," *London Review of Books* blog (July 9, 2012).

Paumgarten, Nick, "Big Shot," *New Yorker* website (September 11, 2011).

Perotta, Tom, "Spin Doctors," *Atlantic* (July 1, 2006).

Rubin, Jon, "Bring Back the Wood," *New York Times* (September 8, 2002).

Smith, Ed, "The Last Days of Roger Federer," *New Statesman* (October 21, 2013).

Yandell, John, "Roger Federer and the Evolution of the Modern Forehand," www.tennisplayer.net (2006).